Pint-sized
IRELAND

in search of the
perfect Guinness

914·15

Evan McHugh

summersdale

Pint-sized
IRELAND

914.15

Pint-sized Ireland

First published by Thomas C. Lothian Pty Ltd, Australia in 2001.

This edition published in 2005 by Summersdale Publishers Ltd.

Summersdale Publishers Ltd
46 West Street
Chichester
West Sussex
PO19 1RP
UK

www.summersdale.com

Printed and bound in Great Britain.

ISBN 1 84024 054 7

ACKNOWLEDGEMENTS

This book couldn't have happened without the kind and generous assistance of a number of people. Sandra Willett at Bord Fáilte and Michelle Armstrong from the Northern Ireland Tourism Board provided invaluable support, information and guidance. Any errors of fact remaining are because I didn't ask, not that they didn't know.

My Australian editor Sarah Dawson combined encouragement, enthusiasm and editorial discipline with remarkable calm in the face of deadlines. The whole team at Summersdale have been a pleasure to work with – patient, creative, professional – qualities I'm still aspiring to.

In Ireland, Pat, Ciaran, Winnie and their friends were the best introduction to the country and its people I could have asked for. And of course, I owe a huge debt and thanks to Michelle/ Twidkiwodm for just about everything.

CONTENTS

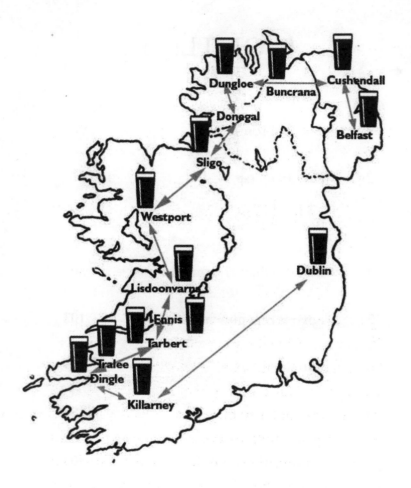

THE FIRST ROUND

It's generally accepted that there's a time and a place for everything. However, it follows that there is also a right time but a wrong place for everything, a wrong time but a right place and, worst of all, a wrong time and a wrong place. When you think about it, life tends to cycle through these four possible combinations and there's actually precious little you can do about it. In fact, there's usually only a one in four chance that here and now is also the right time and place. Which explains why most of the time (75 per cent by my calculations) we end up regretting our actions. Or is that just me?

As it happens, regret is the word that best describes my first experience of Guinness, the black Irish beverage that is considered by those who are being generous as 'an acquired taste'. To someone like me, an Australian raised on Vegemite (which is also described as an acquired taste but regarded by the rest of the world as 'utterly inedible' and 'unspeakably vile') such language is usually regarded as code for 'be afraid, be very afraid'.

Another term the Irish use to describe Guinness is 'moother's milk'. Considering it resembles liquid coal capped with a layer of densely packed froth of a colour one normally associates with festering swamps, one can only conclude that Mother hasn't been well.

So THERE I was on a ferry sailing across the Irish Sea while accompanied by the-woman-I-didn't-know-I-would-one-day-marry (also known as Twidkiwodm for short). Twidkiwodm is actually pronounced Michelle, which is every bit as logical as the pronunciation of the place we were headed for. Our attempts to buy ferry tickets to Dun Laoghaire had already provided ample amusement at the ticket booth in Wales. Come to think of it, we'd been laughed at from end to end of that land of glottal scarring as well, especially around Dolgellau and Ffestiniog. So you know, Dun Laoghaire isn't pronounced Done-La-Gare (that's tourist French for 'I have seen the train station'). It's pronounced Done-Leery (tourist Gaelic for 'I have seen a pervert').

More importantly, with the strangely named ferry port on the outskirts of Dublin starting to peek over a misty horizon, we decided the time had come to acquire a taste for Guinness and to do it pretty bloody fast. The reason was simple enough. We had phoned a couple of Irish mates we knew in Dublin to let them know we were coming.

'Grand,' Pat had enthused. 'We'll take you out and show you the best poobs in town.'

Having had Pat and his mate Ciaran come to stay with us in Sydney, we knew 'the best' probably meant 'most of'. Their visit had been marked by torrential rain that totally contradicted the image Sydney likes to present of having a perfect climate. For two weeks it poured down in biblical proportions, leaving the boys with little option but to seek out the Irish equivalent of an ark (pronounced pub) and engage in time-honoured indoor activities which largely comprised consuming great quantities of Guinness and deriding it as the worst they'd ever tasted.

'It's not the same,' they chorused almost continuously, stoutly refusing to touch the local lagers which they summarily dismissed as 'cat's piss'.

'It moosn't travel well.' Considering Guinness is actually brewed under licence in Australia and has never seen the 'mootherland', they may have had a point. From my perspective it was neither here nor there. I'd found Guinness, which is a stout, so unpalatable after the crisp, clear lagers I was used to that I simply took their word for it. That is, until I found myself on the Irish Sea.

I was headed for their home turf, so to speak, confronting the realisation that I was about to set foot in a place where Guinness was the drink of choice. So I had to acquire a taste for it asap. As the ferry chugged west from Holyhead, I believed that there was a one in four chance that the moment to do so had arrived. The ferry had a bar. It sold Guinness. The time was now.

'Two pints of Guinness, please,' I said with far more confidence than I felt.

The conductor Sir Thomas Beecham once opined that you should try everything once except incest and folk-dancing. Had Tom been beside me on that ferry, he may well have cast his net a little wider. Nevertheless, I took his advice to heart and when I had two pints of the sinister-looking brew in hand, I navigated back to where Twidkiwodm was waiting. I set the glasses down on the table between us and slid into a seat. We sat for a moment steeling ourselves to 'acquire' a taste for Guinness. We may have proposed a little toast at this point. We may have simply said, 'Well, here goes.' I can't remember because what happened next pretty well eclipsed whatever happened immediately before. Sensitive readers may want to skip a page or two at this point, while I explain to those who are made of sterner stuff that the place where you'll taste worse food than airline food is on a ferry. I suspect it's because ferry people know that motion sickness on a boat is worse than that in a plane, so anything they prepare usually spends far less time in their customers' stomachs. What's the point of going to a lot of trouble?

That's why choosing a ferry for our first taste of Guinness was a classic right time, wrong place situation. I know this now. Wrong. Very, very wrong. The taste was of something that had died a horrible death and then been consigned to a cremation that had somehow failed to complete its task of reducing the remains to ash. Perhaps if you scrub down a truly rank barbecue and add water to the scrapings, you might happen upon the recipe for the contents of that glass. For a horrifying moment I suspected there had been a terrible misunderstanding of my pronunciation and what I had actually asked for was whatever they could pump out of the ferry's bilge. Suddenly I was sure I knew where James Joyce got the inspiration for his description of those damned in hell in *A Portrait of the Artist as a Young Man*. He'd drunk Guinness on this ferry.

'Gggg gggg. Ggg,' I said. And I meant it.

It was beyond terrible. It was uber-vile. And in this opinion I was not alone. Twidkiwodm's face had twisted into an expression like a cat's arse. She'd developed a nervous twitch and her skin appeared to ripple through forty shades of green before turning as grey as the water sliding past the window outside.

'Maybe this is the real reason so many of the Irish fled the place,' I said.

'To be shrrr,' Twidkiwodm agreed in a thick Irish brogue. It was some minutes before the effect wore off and she was able to speak with an Australian accent once more.

14

Meanwhile, we seriously considered revising our plans. We had aimed to spend three weeks in Ireland but there was a ferry heading back to Wales the next morning. The problem was that we were going to be met by two Irishmen waiting at the end of the ferry's gangplank, ready to whisk us away for a night to remember no matter how hard we tried to forget it. We were going to have to walk the plank. Unless, of course, we hid until the ferry returned to Wales.

At the time we had no way of knowing that what we had just consumed was far and away the worst Guinness probably in the entire world. For all we knew, what we'd just tasted was perfectly normal. That's why we dreaded what was going to happen when Pat and Ciaran offered us their hospitality. They were going to make us drink more of this stuff and they wouldn't be taking 'no' for an answer.

Under the circumstances we had no choice but to continue acquiring a taste. We lifted our pints, although by now we preferred the term poisoned chalices, and proceeded to drink with every fibre of our will until the glasses were empty, hoping that at some point we would find the key to enjoying this horrible concoction. I suspect that if there ever was a key, that liquid had long since eaten it away.

AT THE HARBOUR of Dun Laoghaire, on the south side of Dublin, we experienced the luck of the Irish: the Irish boys weren't there. We looked for them but only found a bus that was heading for the local youth hostel, so milled around with two fellow travellers who had also come across on the ferry. One was a German girl named Katrin, whom we had met the night before at the youth hostel in Caernarfon; the other was an American cyclist named TJ. We had taken TJ's luggage to the ferry on a bus while he rode his bike. On the ferry, for reasons that were not made clear, cyclists were segregated from the other passengers. In fact there was a sign that read 'Passengers to the right; dogs and cyclists to the left'. It was an interesting lumping together of categories. I had a mental picture of a bunch of cyclists in skin-tight outfits, hunched on all fours alongside the dogs, trying to sniff each other's bums.

At the ferry terminal we hesitated for a while, trying to decide what to do, but the bus was itching to go. There was still no sign of the boys, so we decided to make sure of our first night's accommodation. The fact that we might be avoiding a confrontation with a certain alcoholic libation had nothing to do with it. Well, not much.

As it happened, once we were at the youth hostel another phone call revealed that the boys had been waiting outside the ferry terminal. We'd driven out the gates and gone straight past them. Gosh darn it. This put a slight dent in their plans for the evening, but unfortunately they were not derailed. The fact that the youth hostel had an 11.30 curfew was not insurmountable either.

'Y' moit as well spend the noit dere, now you're booked in,' Pat said. 'But that doosn't mean we can't go drinkin'. It's yer first noit in Dooblin. We'll be round after tea to take y' to a few places.'

He hung up before I could say 'No, no, don't go to any trouble.'

Meanwhile, Twidkiwodm and TJ had started cooking a meal, so I asked Katrin if she wanted to come outside and play frisbee. I always carry one as a compact form of instant entertainment. Or, more exactly, a compact form of entertainment for consenting adults, which won't get them arrested or scare the horses. Now, if you've ever played frisbee with a dog you'll know they tend to slobber on the frisbee quite a lot. But as Katrin leapt, caught, then threw the frisbee back, I was doing quite a bit of slobbering myself. She was gorgeous, and she was an independent traveller. Was I entertaining romantic notions? Arf, arf. Woof.

'And what did the-woman-you-didn't-know-you-would-one-day-marry think of this while she was cooking dinner?' I hear you ask. At the time Twidkiwodm and I were having what we described as an ongoing non-relationship – now a relationship, then a friendship – so playing frisbee with a beautiful German woman wasn't a problem unless, perhaps, it led to something else. It's a bit like the reason Mormons never have sex standing up. It might lead to dancing. Or maybe not.

WHEN PAT SHOWED up he was on his 'Pat Malone' as he put it, although that isn't his last name. He took us to his car, telling us he planned to meet Ciaran in town. 'Coz we don't have mooch toim, we'll only be takin' ye to a few places,' he said.

Pat was exactly like you would imagine an Irish Patrick to be. He had red hair, a red moustache, and a weather-beaten complexion despite being in his early thirties. His mouth was the most animated part of him. At all times it was either laughing, smiling, telling jokes or drinking and despite a prodigious capacity for the latter, he looked in robust health.

As he drove he pointed out the sights along the way. To be honest, there wasn't much to see. We were passing through Dublin's outer suburbs and the houses were pretty much like houses everywhere. There were rows of terraces and housing estates, there was very little that was over two storeys high and most buildings were either painted white or coated in pebbledash, a kind of pebbly brown concrete that can be more accurately described as 'depressing'.

On the midst of the houses, Pat stopped. 'We'll have a drink here,' he said.

The pub looked like the houses. The architecture was, to say the least, undistinguished; it didn't exude the magic that you see in every picture of a traditional Irish pub, which we'd assumed were typical of every licensed premises in the country. Of course, you shouldn't judge a book by its cover (if you don't believe me, just keep reading), but I assumed there was a reason Pat had stopped, and that it would be revealed once we stepped inside. I was wrong.

There were two blokes sitting on cheap stools propping up the bar.

'So what's so special about this place?' I asked.

'Nootin',' Pat replied, and ordered three pints

of Guinness. 'It's joost that it's toim for soom of the gargle.'

We found a seat away from the other drinkers (which wasn't difficult) and attempted to prepare ourselves. 'We tried this stuff on the ferry over,' I explained.

'Oh. You shouldn't a doon that,' Pat replied without hesitation.

'Why's that?'

'It's fookin' shite, that's why. Now get that into ya. We've a lotta poobs ahead of us.'

The fact that 'a few' had become 'a lotta' was the least of our problems. As recent graduates from the school of 'once bitten, twice shy', we approached the pints set before us with the trepidation we felt they deserved. We drank. We swallowed. We waited.

'There now. Dat didn't kill ya, did it?' Pat said.

'No, but the afterburners haven't kicked in yet,' Twidkiwodm answered hesitantly.

Hmm.

We smacked our lips and tongues, warily savouring the flavour. Among her many virtues, Twidkiwodm has quite a refined palate and she is very particular about the taste of things. Another sip.

I didn't want to get too excited yet, but there was the creaminess I'd heard about, mixed with the complex roasted flavours of a true stout. And the flavour lingered long after the swallow, prolonging the experience – which, if you were enjoying it, made it that much better. Even so, these are confronting things for your standard Australian lager drinker, accustomed to a refreshing ale with mouth-cleansing characteristics. And yet... not bad, I thought. Not bad at all.

'Mmm,' Twidkiwodm agreed, a little more circumspect.

'Good then,' Pat said. 'Drink oop and we'll be on our way.'

We did as instructed and while the experience didn't kill us we couldn't be sure whether it had made us stronger. But I couldn't help asking, 'Is the Guinness here special in any way?'

'Not that I know of,' Pat replied. 'Boot we'll be goin' to a few places where the stoof is renowned.'

Pat led. We followed. I didn't know it but our search for the perfect Guinness had begun.

IGNORANCE REALLY IS bliss. George Orwell knew what he was talking about when he wrote *1984*. The best

thing about ignorance is the joy of discovering things you didn't know. Once, while visiting a farm, I went out with a friend to pick some asparagus for dinner. 'What are you doing?' my friend asked as I wandered about looking for a tree or a bush. 'Where do you think it grows?' she asked. 'No idea,' I replied. I was pleasantly surprised to discover that it sprouts from the ground. My knowledge of the world had increased and I felt enriched.

Dublin was like asparagus. I have to confess that I entered the city centre with a sublime lack of knowledge of Irish history, points of interest and significant historical figures. I knew a little bit about its literature, enough to know that it had once been a pretty grim place. And I knew you could write a book like *Angela's Ashes* every twenty years or so and get rich off all the people who think that you are the first to write about Irish hardship.

Other than that, my information base was confined to the usual clichés about forty shades of green, leprechauns and major events like the famine, Irish Diaspora and the Troubles. It was limited to the things that make the news on the opposite side of the planet. I knew I had an Irish connection on my father's side, but no details and no relatives to look up. So, as we drove around looking for a parking spot, I was a clean slate upon which Dublin and the rest of the place could start etching impressions. Like: there's nowhere to park. What I also noticed as we cruised the city centre was the sky. At first I couldn't understand why I thought that was significant, then I realised: even in the centre of town, Dublin is built to a human scale, two or three storeys mostly, so the streets let the sky in. One of the consequences is that church spires still have a dominant position in the cityscape.

The buildings themselves were a mixture of elegant and run-down shopfronts, banks and businesses. The old was shoulder to shoulder with the new and not-so-new, with occasional vacant blocks in between. It all gave an impression, like most old cities, that the place wasn't quite finished or, more correctly, had been subject to gradual change for centuries. Eventually time will erase the bad ideas, retaining the good ones but keeps throwing up a mixture of both in a conglomeration that blights and blesses.

WHEN WE FINALLY found a place to park, Pat pointed out the pub where we would be meeting Ciaran, then led us in the opposite direction. 'He won't be dere yet. And I woont to show ya woon of Oirland's most famous poobs,' he said.

It was just a couple of streets away. 'This is a real poob. Not woon o' yer tourist joints,' Pat explained. He showed us Hartigan's, just off St Stephen's Green, which was more of a shopfront. Around us there were stylish shops and ornate pubs, the kind you see all around the world. This place, on the other hand, was just a pane of glass and an open door. Inside, there was a counter down the middle with a barman on one side and a ragtag collection of old men on the other. As for the décor, the customers seemed to be it. The walls, seats, floor and lighting were a little piece of Dublin that would be forever spartan. In fact, the atmosphere was less that of a pub and more that of a butcher's shop. I was starting to have my doubts about young Pat.

'This is the haunt of many famous writers,' Pat explained. I scanned the customers. None of them looked famous. None of them looked like writers. But you never can tell with famous writers. If someone pointed to a bunch of tired-looking drunks and said they were famous writers, I wouldn't argue with them. I'm not a famous writer either but I did once tell someone I was a writer, and after they'd looked me up and down they called me a liar. (Come to think of it, people who've read my stuff have taken some convincing, too.)

'Which famous writers?' I asked.

'Brendan Behan for woon,' Pat replied as he attracted the barman's attention and ordered three more pints.

I'd heard of him. Allegedly, he was as famous a writer as he was a famous drunk, and I was under the impression that what really set a pub apart was if Behan hadn't drunk there. It might also be set apart if it could pour a beer in less time than it took to write a one-act play. In Hartigan's, the barman poured the Guinnesses about two-thirds full, then left them and went back to the other end of the bar to talk to his mates. Pat didn't seem to notice as a minute, then another, then another, ticked by. He chatted away until he detected that I was looking distractedly over his shoulder to our still unpoured drinks.

'Won't be long now,' he said.

I was dismayed. I'd heard that the Irish were relaxed and easy-going, but this was just plain slack.

'It takes toim to pour a good Guinness,' Pat explained. 'It has to settle before ye toop it oop.'

Sure enough, the barman came back and topped up each glass, then topped it up again. Satisfied, he put them on the bar in front of us. At last. The whole operation had taken a good five minutes. In most parts of the world the riot would have started around the three-minute mark.

As it happens, the wait was worth it. This was the best Guinness we had tasted so far, although its competition was not what you would call 'fierce'.

A brewer of my acquaintance once told me that a lot of beers are subjected to so much research and development that they inevitably become utterly mediocre. They get analysed by so many focus groups that they end up having no taste at all – that way they don't offend anyone. Where Guinness is concerned, I was starting to think of Hermann Hesse's line: not for everybody. It certainly wasn't everyone's cup of tea. Me? After a couple of decent pints of the stuff, it was starting to go down quite easily.

IT WAS TIME to go and find Ciaran. Pat led us around to the pub he'd pointed out earlier, O'Donoghue's. Now this was more like it. The place was packed with people jostling and chatting at full volume in a smoky room full of mirrors and noise. There were several members of staff keeping busy behind the bar, which was covered in half-empty pints of Guinness. Or were they half-full?

'This is nootin',' Pat said, trying to spot Ciaran as we squeezed through the throng. 'When it's really busy, they've a bloke stand on the bar. You shout yer order and they pass the drinks and mooney over people's heads.'

We managed to find a place against the wall furthest from the bar where we could scan the crowd. We couldn't see Ciaran anywhere. Pat was off to get some more drinks. As it happened, Twidkiwodm and I were a bit taller than most of the customers, so we could get a pretty good view of the room. From our vantage point above the crowd I could clearly see what took place next. After Pat placed his order the barman grabbed one of the half-empty glasses, put it under the tap and started filling it. I nudged Twidkiwodm (she's the same height as me, although we don't always see eye to eye). 'Yes, I saw it too,' she said. 'Perhaps it's a quaint local custom.'

'Bugger quaint. It's disgusting.'

Patrick came back with the pints.

'We saw them filling half-empty glasses,' I said, appalled.

27

'Dey do it to speed tings oop,' Pat replied. He was having to do a lot of explaining. 'They keep a few waitin' to toop oop the rest o' the way.'

Aah. Half-full or half-empty depends on whether the glass is being filled or emptied. I wasn't sure if it was very Zen or very Irish. It was about halfway through this pint that a voice at my side said, 'I see you've found the gargle den.'

Gargle den?

It was Ciaran. Since we hadn't been able to find him, he'd snuck up on us. He gave me a smile and a firm handshake. 'Welcome to Oirland,' he said warmly.

Describing Ciaran is easy because he looks a bit like Bruce Willis, only more brooding. He's fairly solidly built and looks like he wouldn't come out worst if there was ever any trouble. Even more than Pat, he was the reason we'd needed to acquire a taste for Guinness. We didn't want any trouble.

By the gargle, I presumed he meant the Guinness. I held up my glass. 'Yes,' I said. 'Pat's been teaching us.'

'Grand,' he said, noticing Twidkiwodm as well. 'Ond I see y've brought yer mot.'

'My what?'

'Yer mot: Michelle, yer best girl.'

He leaned over to kiss her on the cheek. He was particularly impressed that she was not only drinking Guinness but drinking it in pints.

'You know I don't do things by halves,' Twidkiwodm replied. Which was just as well.

We had another pint in the back bar where some musicians were playing – a violin, an accordion – while the boys mapped out the next couple of days. They were particularly keen on the next night and a 'proper poob crawl'. And as luck would have it, the coming weekend was a bank holiday. That meant the boys could show us the west coast and even more pubs.

While we were talking a couple of young blokes got up and started singing with the musicians. After a while the musicians stopped but the lads just kept singing. The people in the pub encouraged them, even though one of them sounded like he'd spent the money his mum gave him for singing lessons on something else. To keep his confidence up during the song, his mate reached over, gripped his hand and held it while they tackled the tough notes together.

At the end, the crowd clapped and cheered. As they started another song I looked around at the crowd. I had a pint of Guinness in my hand, a group of friends around me and there was music in the air. It was the sort of clichéd scene you see in tourist brochures, except it was real. And it was only our first night in town. Was it possible that the Irish tourism spin doctors, faced with a lack of palm-tree-lined tropical lagoons bathed in glaringly bright sunshine, had resorted to actually showing people what their country was really like? The cunning sods.

THE NEXT PUB we went to has a name I can't remember. This may have had something to do with the previous four pints. I think it was somewhere on the northside and I'm sure it was painted black and gold on the outside, which narrows things down only slightly. I do know, because they told me, that we were getting into the boys' usual stamping ground. However, this pub wasn't their local – they were planning to take us there the next night.

One thing Pat and Ciaran had told me while they were in Australia was that 'all the women in Ireland are beautiful'. At the time I thought they were just boasting. In this pub, though, I was starting to realise they weren't straying too far from the truth. Several of the women in this place could easily have gotten jobs as angels. What really caught me was the eyes – the most striking grey-blue. And they didn't just glance at you: they looked right at you, right into you, with a mixture of interest and self-confidence.

The next surprise was that these angels were friendly. When one of them came up and asked if anyone was sitting on the barstool beside us, Ciaran replied 'Yes, you are.'

She took it as an invitation to join us, soon found out all about us and was pleased to see we were not only drinking the local stout but also visiting her country. 'It's a woonderful place. I'm sure you'll have a great toim.'

It turned out that this pub also had literary connections, in the form of poetry recitals.

'Tomorrow, you'll be meetin' a friend of ours named Dinger,' Pat told me. 'He's a wroiter loik you. A poet.'

'What sort of poetry?'

'Hard to say,' he replied. 'But in this very poob, he resoited woon of 'em. It wasn't poetry noit, but he stood on the bar and shouted that he had a poem he wanted to resoit. Eventually, the place went quoiet so he could be heard. Then he says, "Me poem is called Soilence." Everywoon's listenin'. Dinger stonds dere for a moment, for emphasis loik. Den he says, "Tankyou".'

I almost snorted Guinness out of my nose. 'What did they do to him?'

'Dey clapped. He's very clever is our man Dinger.'

'He sounds like a fookin' eejit,' the beautiful girl said, introducing us to the disconcerting use of language that characterised even the angels. The Irish just don't seem to be as precious as other cultures when it comes to swearing. And of course, on the lips of an angel it ends up sounding like poetry anyway. Or is that just me? Or the Guinness?

It was getting late. The pub was near to closing time and so was the hostel near Dun Laoghaire where we were supposed to be staying. We started pressing the boys about the time, which only produced another round of drinks. Eventually they relented and we headed into the night. Along the way, though, we stopped for a nightcap at a bar they spotted, which meant we were half an hour late at the hostel. It was totally dark as we drove into the square where Katrin and I had played frisbee. It wasn't looking good.

'Looks deserted,' Pat said, and we started considering how we could spend the night at Ciaran's place and come back for our luggage in the morning.

Just then, a shadowy head appeared in the kitchen. Then someone waved.

'Signs of movement,' Twidkiwodm said. 'We're in.'

The people who ran the place opened up. 'Sorry,' they said. 'We thought you'd be mooch longer or we'd have torned on the loits. Coom in ond have a wee soomthin'.'

It turned out they'd been waiting for us, quietly sipping whiskey in the dark. We were starting to suspect we weren't going to meet many teetotallers in Ireland. If there are any, they must be distinctly lonely.

2

Dublin on tap

Our first full day in Ireland dawned without hangovers. Under the circumstances, it was nothing short of a miracle. We could still feel the pints from the night before sloshing around but we didn't have the usual nausea, splitting headache, or alcohol-oozing-out-of-every-pore feeling. What we had may have been the feeling babies have when they drink too much 'moother's milk'. However, not knowing how big Dubliners are on Freudian psychology, we thought it best not to explore that notion further.

We had breakfast at the hostel, then spilled out into the street with the other guests. TJ cycled off and Katrin came with us on the bus into the city. We said goodbye to her at the bus terminus (some more reluctantly than others) and went our separate ways. Twidkiwodm and I had arranged to meet the boys in town but we had some time to kill, so we checked out O'Connell Street, Dublin's main thoroughfare. Our guidebook was fairly dismissive about it, which struck me as a bit unfair, although my opinion may have been coloured by the fact I was seeing the city in broad daylight for the first time. Like most travellers I tend to want to get a good first impression from any place I've decided to visit. Otherwise it's Dear Diary, day one: damn it. I knew we should have gone somewhere with palm-lined lagoons.

O'Connell Street, which I'll call a fine boulevard for the time being, had several statues of various figures in the Irish pantheon. At least I think they were. I have to admit some left me wondering what dictionary they'd used for the definition of the word 'fame'. The one of Catholic nationalist Daniel O'Connell made sense. So did the ones of various other martyrs for the Irish cause. But the statue of the bloke who put Dublin's water on was pretty doubtful. He had a name, but it's disappeared down the S-bend of forgotten information along with all the other pioneers of sewerage I've ever heard of.

Then I discovered O'Connell Street doesn't just have one statue with aquatic associations. It's got two. Maybe the Irish have a thing about fluids, which might explain why they've erected a statue with the Liffey, the river that flows through the city, as its subject. It's called the Anna Livia Millennium Fountain and it was commissioned to mark the 1,000 years since the Vikings settled what became the city of Dublin. As milestones go, 1,000 is pretty significant. So it's reasonable to expect something special as a memorial. To be honest, Anna looks like the sculptor caught her at a bad moment, but she does provide two valuable lessons for sculptors:

1.   Think very carefully before agreeing to do a sculpture of a waterway.

2.   A reclining figure may be the goods, but a figure lying in the bath is really stretching things.

Locals dismiss the work as 'the floozie in the jacuzzi', and yet, had Irish Olympic swimmer Michelle Smith won the backstroke, they would have had a statue ready-made. Who'd have been any the wiser?

While we're on the subject of incomprehensible art, James Joyce was pretty big on Anna Livia as well.

There's a passage in *Finnegans Wake* called 'Anna Livia Plurabelle', which uses the names of hundreds of rivers plus a few lakes to tell the story. The passage reportedly took Joyce 1,600 hours to write, but I suspect it takes the average reader a lot longer to understand it.

HAVING STUDIED ONE of Dublin's smaller enigmas, we went to find the boys at the telephone exchange where they worked, which was also on O'Connell Street. We thought we were just going to drop our bags with them and then head off sightseeing, but Pat had other plans.

'Come wit me,' he said, and disappeared into the labyrinth of the exchange.

If you ever get the chance to see inside a telephone exchange, grab it. It's nothing like what you'd expect, unless for some reason you'd expect to see a dinosaur's entrails from inside the actual dinosaur. We were surrounded by coiling coloured tubes and cables as we burrowed through narrow passages until, in a distant corner, Pat stopped beside a very ordinary-looking phone.

'What's your parents' phone noomber?' he asked.

I told him and he said, 'Roit. When dat phone

rings, answer it.' Then he disappeared.

We waited for a couple of minutes and sure enough, the thing rang.

'Hello.'

'Evan?'

'Dad!' Pat had put a call through to Australia.

'Where are you son? What time is it?' he asked.

'I'm in Dublin. It's 10.30 a.m.'

'Top of the mornin' to ya,' he replied without missing a beat.

We talked for quite a while, courtesy of Irish Telecom. In relating this story I realise I could get Pat into trouble. Accordingly I considered changing his name to something that would make him untraceable. But when I realised the most common Irish name I could think of was Patrick, I gave up.

Shortly after we left the phone exchange, in fact only a block down O'Connell Street, we ran straight into Katrin. She was just coming out of a place called the Kylemore Café.

If you've ever met someone you feel destined to get to know better, that's what I'd felt about Katrin when we first met in Wales. I couldn't help thinking there was some kind of relationship we were meant to explore. Actually, I'd felt the same way about

Twidkiwodm when I first met her. I'd immediately had the feeling we'd be friends, if not lovers, for years. Perhaps that's why we took each other a bit for granted: we were so sure of each other there was no need to be possessive. But Twidkiwodm isn't the sort of person who'll stand by while you make a move on a stranger, destiny or no destiny. So, after a little while, we went our separate ways.

'Fancy meeting Katrin like that,' I said as we headed in the direction of the Liffey. Actually, I was wondering if I hadn't broken some kind of record, having landed in a love triangle in a new country in under a day. 'Do you think it's Kismet?'

'I doubt it,' Twidkiwodm replied, seemingly preoccupied with the guidebook. 'I think that's in Turkey.'

WE'D JUST SAVED a fortune on phone-calls, so we were more than ready to pay the anticipated fee at the first proper sight we wanted to see, the Ha'penny Bridge. It sounded like a bargain. To our pleasant surprise they haven't been charging any fee at all since 1919.

Built in 1816 for pedestrians, the Ha'penny was originally named after the Duke of Wellington, who was born in Dublin. The name was eventually changed perhaps because, when he was teased about his Irish birthplace, he is supposed to have replied, 'Being born in a stable does not make one a horse.'

The bridge also gave us our first glimpse of the much-vaunted Liffey. Here was the stream to which odes had been written and sculptures carved, one of the city's great founts of inspiration. So we stood in the middle of the bridge and looked down with appropriate awe. There was a mass of swirling grey murk sweeping quickly past. Almost as quickly our awe gave way to the feeling that the Anna Livia Fountain was looking better all the time.

Perhaps we needed to be on the bridge on a cold dark night, when it was more atmospheric. I could see myself wrapped in a long coat, collar turned up to ward off the chill, my face occasionally lit by the glow from a cigarette. Snakes of light were slithering towards me on the surface of the river.

There was a noise in the shadows and a figure hurried onto the bridge, cloak billowing behind. It was Twidkiwodm.

'I can't stay long,' she whispered breathlessly. 'I said I was going to buy cigarettes.'

We embraced, our lips pressing together in a moment that seemed to last forever.

'Come with me,' I said. 'We'll run away to the Civil War.'

'Which one?'

'I don't know. There must be one somewhere.'

'I couldn't. It's too dangerous,' she said. 'But don't let me stop you. Go. Go and see the world. Forget about me. Forget about us. Just remember the way we are, here, right now... and the Liffey. Never forget the Liffey.'

Somewhere, someone was playing 'Stairway to Heaven' on the piano accordion.

I turned and saw Twidkiwodm putting a ha'penny, maybe more, into a busker's hat. She gave me a hurry-up look.

Reluctantly, I followed.

ON THE OTHER side of the bridge we made our way through the pubs and restaurants of Temple Bar to the entrance to Trinity College. I may not have known much about Ireland but I knew about this place. Or, more accurately, I knew about two of its former students and one of its books.

The first former student, Jonathan Swift, was something of a rarity among famous Irish writers in that he actually lived and wrote in Ireland. Most of the others, like Joyce, have tended to shoot through and then rhapsodise or bitch about the place from afar. Swift was born in Dublin in 1667, went to England in 1689 to pursue a political career, but when that was a fizzer he returned to Ireland and took to religion. He also turned his pen to political satire and instead of bitching about Ireland he bitched about the English.

When I was about 13 or 14, an English teacher read my class a satirical essay of Swift's called 'A Modest Proposal'. In it he suggested that the English landlords take to eating Irish babies, since they'd committed every other imaginable atrocity upon the place. It may be one of the earliest examples of 'biting satire'. At any rate, I've never forgotten it, particularly because the language was direct and neither scholarly nor smug.

The writings of the other former student, Samuel Beckett, aren't smug either. They're just weird. After studying at Trinity in the 1920s, Beckett nicked off to France in the thirties where, with other exponents of the Theatre of the Absurd, he deconstructed the traditional form of the play to highlight the futility of human existence. He may not have been the inspiration for Eeyore in *Winnie-the-Pooh* or the

Hemulen in *Finn Family Moomintroll,* but if he was it wouldn't surprise me at all. His best-known play *Waiting for Godot* isn't giving the plot away, since there isn't one, to reveal that Godot never shows up. Like all good Irish plays (especially ones like Godot, which was first written in French), there was a riot when it was first performed, revolving around whether it was a work of genius or total crap. The best description of it is that it's a two-act play in which nothing happens, twice. It also inspired a piece of graffiti that reads: 'Back in five minutes. Godot.'

Nevertheless, in 1969 Sam won the Nobel Prize in Literature but true to form he refused to go to Stockholm and collect it. Instead, the Swedes were treated to a performance of Waiting for Beckett. Clearly, Beckett's art imitated his recalcitrant nature.

At Trinity, a guided tour included a visit to the third item I was interested in, so we decided it was worth the price of a ticket. The Book of Kells is perhaps the greatest treasure in all Ireland, the work of monks who fled to Kells (just outside Dublin) in the eighth century to escape the raids of Vikings. In it, the four gospels are illustrated by hand in exquisite detail: it's remarkable, and no matter how closely you look there's hardly any crossing out at all.

When the guide finally turned up for the tour, he had a distinctly un-Irish inflection. He told us he was from Melbourne, Australia, but had been a student at Trinity for a couple of years. It made about as much sense as someone from Denmark conducting tours of the Sydney Opera House but at least we could understand what he said.

Then we got to the Treasury. If you love old books, really love them, go now, book a ticket to Ireland, and visit the Old Library in the Treasury of Trinity College, Dublin. Yes, the Treasury contains the Book of Kells in a glass case surrounded by people politely jostling for a look at the page that is open for that day. But after a nun elbowed me in the ribs I wandered upstairs to take a look at the rest of the place. That's when I found the Old Library, perhaps the most beautiful room in the world. In front of me, row upon row, shelf upon shelf reaching up to an arched ceiling two storeys high, were crammed with beautifully bound antiquarian books. When Twidkiwodm found me, all I could do was whisper 'Look at this place.'

The shelves were roped off from riff-raff such as me, but I would have given anything to reach out to a book at random and snatch a few moments hearing its author's ancient voice. Then we found a bust of

Jonathan Swift at the end of one of the shelves. It was a bit like meeting a friend.

Among the other items on display was an aged harp once thought to have belonged to Irish chieftain Brian Boru before it was used for the harp trademark of Guinness. There's also a copy of the Declaration of Independence that was issued during the Easter Rising of 1916. It was a little tattered, having survived street battles, the failure of the rising and the execution of the ringleaders. Then it had set in chain events that created a nation. Not bad for a tattered sheet of paper. While I read it a few people wandered up from the Book of Kells, glanced at the books and went back downstairs. They didn't know what they were missing. I couldn't help feeling the Book of Kells was only the tip of Ireland's literary heritage at the Treasury. Upstairs, there's the whole iceberg.

AFTER THE OLD Library it seemed reasonable to think that we weren't likely to find a finer collection of books for a very long time. But on a tip from Ciaran, we walked over to a place we'd never heard of, the Chester Beatty Library and Gallery of Oriental Art. It was next door to Dublin Castle, but judging from the lack of crowds no one else had heard of it either.

I was starting to have my doubts about Ciaran.

All I can say now is that he may fix phones for a living but he sure knows a hell of a lot about books. Ditto Chester Beatty. It turns out that old Chester was a wealthy industrialist and mining magnate who spent the middle of the twentieth century collecting manuscripts. And none of your tat either. Gallery after gallery had some of the oldest copies of the Koran and the Bible in existence, Babylonian tablets 6,000 years old, Coptic, Japanese, Chinese and Buddhist texts. And then there are galleries of Asian art, especially Japanese. It was the Book of Kells multiplied by about five hundred and my mind started to boggle – that, or my first Guinness was starting to kick in.

We were beginning to feel overwhelmed by all the culture, but there was still one more sight I really wanted to see. The treasures of the National Museum of Ireland had toured Australia a few years before and I'd been so impressed by the intricately worked gold artefacts I'd decided that if I ever went to Ireland I'd go and see what else the museum had to show. Quite a lot, as it happens. For many years it seems to have been a curious Irish custom that whenever they made something really good, they buried it in a peat bog.

This wasn't just odd, it was pointless, since it's another Irish custom to cut peat and burn it for cooking and heating. So a lot of the stuff has been dug up again. Fortunately, many of these treasure hoards have ended up in the National Museum – gold, silver and bronze dating back to thousands of years before Christ. The museum features the Ardagh Chalice (800 AD), the Cross of Cong (1123 AD), the Tara Brooch (eighth century AD) and Bronze Age pieces ranging from 1800 to 800 BC. Like all the things we'd seen in the last twenty-four hours, the treasures on display made an impression on my rapidly evolving understanding of Ireland and the Irish. On the one hand, you could say they were the result of exploiting the masses and come the revolution we'll smelt them down into plowshares, comrade. On the other hand, they're the ultimate technical and cultural refinement of artisans who established beyond doubt that the Irish were never just a bunch of dumb 'paddies'. Either way, after seeing all these sights we were reeling. And we weren't even drunk. At least, not yet.

We decided to take a break and went into a pub across the road from Hartigan's. This one, Hourican's, claimed to have won the James Joyce Award for authentic Irish pubs. It even had a plaque with a quote from *Ulysses* that wondered whether it was possible to walk from one side of Dublin to the other without passing a pub. The real challenge would be finding someone in Dublin who could be bothered trying.

IT WAS GETTING late as we crossed back over the Liffey, passing beggars and bookshops in almost equal numbers. At the steps of the Post Office in O'Connell Street, we bumped into Katrin yet again. She'd found accommodation in a city hostel and as she was still in town we suggested she come out drinking with us that night. Well, *I* suggested it. Twidkiwodm didn't seem to mind. I suspect the prospect of being the lone woman among a pack of drunken Irish and Australian men was fairly daunting.

The Post Office was our last stop before meeting Ciaran for a lift back to his house. The building (since rebuilt) was the centre of the 1916 Rising and the Irish Republic was proclaimed on its steps. The English responded by shelling the place and setting it ablaze, and many of the leaders were caught. Had they simply remained in gaol the Rising may well have fizzled out, as few Irish people had supported it. However, when the English started shooting the rebels they effectively became martyrs and Irish opinion started to turn. The English had badly miscalculated; they may have won the battle but they eventually lost the war.

Inside the PO, paintings depict scenes from the uprising. A lot of it is pretty harrowing stuff, especially if you've just nipped in to post a letter. There's also a sculpture of the legendary Irish warrior Cúchulain, which is dedicated to those who died in 1916. The legend goes that in his last battle he tied himself to a tree so that no matter how badly he was injured he could keep fighting to the end. Even after he was dead his enemies were so scared of him they didn't move in until they saw a raven perch on his shoulder, ready to snack on the legendary warrior. That's the cheerful moment the sculpture captures, although the raven doesn't look like something you'd want to tangle with either.

DRIVING US THROUGH Dublin's suburbs, Ciaran was obviously pleased as we rattled on about everything we'd seen. Ciaran still lived with his mother and father in a neat two-storey house in the city's north (he's since married). When his mum opened the door to us we went through the usual confused ritual of introductions while manoeuvring people and baggage in the confined space at the front door. Gradually we diffused into the lounge.

'Is that all you've got with you?' Mrs Ciaran asked, as I stacked my day pack on top of Twidkiwodm's considerably larger one.

'Evan travels ridiculously light,' Twidkiwodm explained, not happening to mention that I was the mule for her baggage while she lightly shouldered mine.

'Everything you need is in there?' Mrs Ciaran was still rather doubtful.

'For short trips, yes,' I assured her. As guests, I felt it was important we should appear normal. If your host starts thinking 'that bag's only big enough for the severed head of the last fool who gave this maniac a bed' you can find yourself warming a kerb in no time. But I've always travelled light. If I find an appropriate moment I might explain how I manage to travel with minimal luggage, although I suspect it comes from being a writer. All you really need is clean underpants, a notebook and a pen. And there are plenty of writers who'll dispute the underpants.

We settled on the lounge and made awkward conversation with Ciaran's father, a retired member of the Garda, while Mrs Ciaran went to make some tea. To put it mildly, Mr Ciaran wasn't at all shy when it came to expressing his opinions. And his solution to most of the issues he raised was so swift and terrible (and yet remarkably consistent) that it seemed like a good thing he'd retired from the force. While I was making a mental note never to litter anywhere within sight of him, Ciaran's mother came back in and told him to shut up. 'Don't listen to a word he says,' she told us. That was easy for her to say – the marriage vows make reference to love and honour but skip over listening. Without a marriage contract, we feared the penalty for not being attentive.

After a chat over a cuppa and biscuits Mrs Ciaran got up and announced it was time for supper. She opened the doors to the dining room and I rose to follow her. Then I caught sight of the dining table.

'Jesus, Mary and Joseph,' I thought. Had all three suddenly appeared, Ciaran's mum could have fed them for a year. Plates of ham, roast beef, salami, pastrami and chicken jostled with salads and steamed vegetables. There were casseroles and piles of bread (rye, soda, brown, white). Fruit? I've been to places where mangos lie rotting on the ground, they're so plentiful, but there wasn't as much fruit as was piled on this table. Cakes? Several.

We were utterly astounded. You hear stories about Irish hospitality but there was so much food it was almost embarrassing.

'Go on with you. It's no trooble at all.'

'Really. This is just… just… '

'Nonsense,' she said. 'It's my way of saying thanks for looking after the boys in Australia. I'm sure your mothers would do the same.'

She might have been right but I doubt they could do so without organised food drives. Clearly, the table was about something other than just food. So we ate. And ate. And ate. It turned out that thoroughly lining our stomachs was the perfect preparation for what was to come.

THAT NIGHT, THE forces of drinking gathered at Gaffney's, a snug little venue near the pub we'd been to the night before. From the way Pat and Ciaran had described him, we were expecting Dinger to be a bit on the 'different' side. And he was that. He had long, jet-black hair, tied back in a ponytail, a full black beard and piercing blue eyes. His face was thin and his features sharply defined. If you're thinking either Jesus Christ or Rasputin, you may have seen the notes Twidkiwodm and I compared when we had a moment alone. He wore the international uniform of the starving artist – dark shapeless trousers, dark checked shirt, a tattered off-black jacket. Dinger and I had a lot in common. Especially when it came to starving. At the time I'd been a struggling writer for three years.

'I see you're drinkin' de Guinness den,' Dinger half asked rhetorically, half stated, as our first pints arrived.

'We're learning to.' I looked at my first pint for the day and had a speculative taste. Mmm. No shock. No horror. Yet another example of fine Irish craftsmanship.

'Moother's milk,' he said, drinking up. 'Though you'll not be gettin' de best Guinness here in Dooblin.'

'Oh. Where's the best then?'

'De west coontry. Over dere folk still hold on to the old ways. They know a good Guinness ond dey won't put oop wid second best. Here in Dooblin dey'll drink shite. Dat's why dey trook all de best over to de west.'

'Is that a fact?'

'It is dat.'

'Lucky for us we'll be going there in a couple of days.'

'Yer not wrong dere,' he said. 'Den you'll see. And woil yer dere, ye moit be foindin' de poteen.'

'Potcheen?' I asked phonetically.

'Dat's roit, poteen. Dey make it in the woild hills, in illegal stills. It's powerful stoof.'

'We'll keep an eye out for it.' Despite our experience on the ferry I was still prepared to take Thomas Beecham's advice to heart.

'Ye'll be looky,' Dinger retorted. He seemed to enjoy dangling a carrot. 'De people dere keep it well out o' soit. Yer coostems men are always sorchin' for it. Dey've not mooch look.' It sounded like alcohol's answer to a leprechaun.

From this point on, things get a little sketchy. Firstly, because I wasn't taking notes. Secondly, because even if I had been it wouldn't have been long before I lost the ability to write. And thirdly, because quite a bit of what happened was a complete blur. I do remember a sign in Gaffney's that I liked: 'God does not deduct from our lifespan time spent sailing.' After Gaffney's we went to quite a few pubs on Dublin's northside, and some on the southside. Then we headed to the Clock Tavern in Howth, which involved a long drive to the outskirts of town during which we played a game of 'Are we there yet?' 'Shoot oop.' 'Are we there yet?' 'Shoot oop.' 'Are we there yet?' 'Shoot oop.' There was a reason we went to the Clock Tavern. It was one of the few pubs in Ireland that had a beer garden. And the reason for that became obvious pretty quickly. Even the summer nights in Ireland are freezing. There was a bonfire in a steel drum, around which we huddled, slowly rotating our bodies in an effort to keep warm all around. Maybe it would have been warmer if there were more people with us, but all the locals were crowded inside the bar, snug as bugs. Dinger counted himself a local.

While we were at the Clock, the boys made a call to their local pub to make 'soom arrangements'. It was getting late and the pubs were closing. Or so we thought. We dropped Katrin back at her hostel and arrived at the pub just before midnight. Metal shutters were pulled down over the windows and doors and the place was completely dark. 'Deserted' was the word that leapt to mind.

The boys were undaunted. They went up to the shutters and hammered as hard as they could. In a lull between hammerings, I found that if I pressed my ear to a shutter I could faintly make out the sound of many voices. A passer-by wouldn't have heard a thing.

The boys resumed their battery and were ahead on points when I finally heard a voice from within say 'Quoi-et. Soomwoon's bangin' on de dorr.'

There was a hush within, then the shutter rose a bit and a voice said 'Who's dere?'

'Pat and Ciaran. We rang orrlier.'

'Roit,' the voice said, lifting the shutter. 'In ye coom. Be quick.'

We piled into a room that was, well, full of people. It was also quiet, but that changed as soon as the publican closed the shutter.

'Welcome to Oirland,' he shouted to us. 'What'll ye have?'

Pat and Ciaran got the first round. Two pints of Guinness for each of us, two halves for Twidkiwodm, who was starting to understand why less was more. Plus two shots of whiskey each. It turned out that what kept the bar open was a prodigious consumption of alcohol.

A sense of honour dictated that I try to match the boys glass for glass. This was, of course, a big mistake. We hadn't finished what was before us when the barman shouted,

'Last drinks! Ladies and gentlemen! Last drinks!'

There was a general movement towards the bar. My round and the boys said, 'Same again.' Two pints each, two whiskeys each. Two halves and two whiskeys for Twidkiwodm, to go with the half and the whiskey she hadn't touched.

'I take it they can't throw us out until we finish our drinks.'

'Roit.'

While I waited at the bar I checked the place out. It was a real local. Everyone looked like they knew everyone else. Most of the seating was what you'd find in the lounge-room of someone's home. I can remember the name of this pub well but you really don't want to go there. Not because it struck me as a place that would be hostile to strangers, but Ciaran had pointed out one fella and told me he'd got out of an eight-year gaol sentence during an amnesty. 'Dey'd put him in after dey'd found enough explosives in his house to blow up Dooblin.'

'Last drinks!'

Half an hour later, more Guinness and more whiskey. I was sure I could feel my liver swelling.

'Last drinks!' The table was covered in drinks. We were swimming in the stuff.

For some reason I feel I should insert a message in here about responsible consumption of alcohol. Except at the time the messenger was almost under the table. And I'm sure the crowd in that pub would have laughed at such notions. They didn't seem to be getting drunk at all. Me? No question. I was drunk. Twidkiwodm was only marginally better. It was around 3 a.m. that the place finally chucked us out. And not a moment too soon.

When the Irish play, they play hard: 'the craic' they call it. They use it for anything that involves having a good time, as in 'Damn foin craic'. At 3 a.m., however, it can equally refer to cracking under the strain. This is especially the case when you discover you're not going home. 'We're not far from Dinger's,' Pat said. 'His moom woonts to meet ya.'

'At 3 a.m.? Drunk?'

'She's expectin' us,' Dinger added.

I was in no condition to argue. Nor was I in any condition to meet someone's parents. The boys insisted it didn't matter. As we blundered off I hoped they were wrong and that Dinger's parents had long since gone to bed.

DINGER'S MUM WAS ironing. We discovered this as soon as he opened the door to his tiny house and we saw her at the ironing board in the middle of the lounge. Actually, there was a glimpse of a woman with a striking resemblance to Spike Milligan, then we were set upon by the most excitable fox terrier that ever leapt or barked. The crazed dog flew madly around the room as five new people staggered into the cramped space. It kept barking and leaping onto chairs as Dinger's mum, wrapped in a dressing gown, bade us welcome and be seated, and sent her husband, who also looked like Spike Milligan, to open a bottle of wine.

'Oh no,' I said, 'not more alcohol, please.'

'Nooo,' Pat and Ciaran chorused. 'Ye moost troi it. It's alderberry wine. Dinger's moom makes it herself.'

Moments later I was given a glass containing something whose resemblance to wine seemed to stop at the colour. I tried to apologise to Mrs Spike Milligan for coming into her home in a drunken state.

'Nonsense,' she insisted. 'It's not every day we entertain folk from so far away.'

'Nor so far gone,' I thought to myself.

As she talked she continued ironing. I perched on

the arm of a chair and set about exploring the fruit-driven effervescence of young alderberry wine. Alarm signals were emanating from my taste buds. I quickly found myself thankful that I'd perched – Dinger's mum's alderberry wine isn't something you want to try while standing up – but I wrestled my attention away and tuned into the conversation going on around me. I tried to appear sober. I wasn't fooling anybody. And the terrier didn't help. It wouldn't settle down, but instead ricocheted from the floor to chairs to the sideboard, while Dinger's dad kept shouting 'Shoot oop. Shoot the fook oop, ye eejit'.

The eejit leapt to the floor, ran in tight little circles, then raced at Twidkiwodm. She fended it off. Then I noticed the dog slurp some wine out of Dinger's dad's glass. He did nothing to stop it. Suddenly I understood. The dog was drunk. I started to giggle like a fool.

'Shoot oop, ye stoopid mutt. Shoot oop.'

The animal was out of its furry little mind. The quadruped was not alone.

BEER AND POLITICS

The next morning, I didn't have a hangover. It felt like I'd fallen off a cliff. Though my eyes were shut, I deduced from the needles skewering through my eyelids into the depths of my brain that it was daylight. When I actually opened my eyes, matters only got worse. I found that I was completely alone, lying under some blankets on a lounge in a room that was totally unfamiliar.

I looked at my watch. It was 7 o'clock. But was it morning or evening?

Gingerly, I raised myself to a sitting position,

feeling the contents of my head slosh forward as I did so. While that was unpleasant, holding my head upright wasn't much fun either. My face seemed to have developed some kind of magnetic attraction to the pillow. After taking a few moments to summon some energy, I slowly got up and went to the window. Outside there was a tree-lined street, neatly tended gardens, a line of tidy houses. All of which meant nothing to me.

OK. Where was I last night? Yesterday? What city was I in? For the life of me I couldn't remember. When you do a lot of travelling, waking up in a strange place can take a few seconds while you reorient yourself. But this was something else.

I went over and tried the door to the room. Outside there was a corridor with a couple of doorways. All the doors were shut. What was behind them? I was in no shape to go and find out.

I returned to the lounge and took stock. I was sure I'd been drinking some time recently (at least those little hammers pounding in my head had a familiar rhythm). I knew my name, so I didn't have amnesia, but I couldn't remember anything else. My passport was still in a pouch around my neck so I had a look, hoping for clues. I already knew I was an Australian but apart from that there didn't seem to be much to go on. At this point, panic may have been an option but my glands lacked the energy to pump the necessary adrenalin. So, I did the only logical thing. I went back to bed and hoped things would take care of themselves.

THEY DID. AN hour later I heard sounds of movement outside the room so I got up and tottered out. In a kitchen there was a woman I vaguely recognised: Ciaran's mum, making a cup of tea.

'Oh, you're up early. You got in quite late. Did you have a good time?'

Little details were slowly coming back. Such as, I'm in Ireland. 'That moother's milk sure packs a punch,' I said.

She looked at me like I wasn't making any sense. Under the circumstances, who was I to argue?

After a while Twidkiwodm appeared and told me we'd left Dinger's around 4.30 a.m.

'You were in quite a state,' she said.

'Not a lot's changed,' I conceded.

When Ciaran came in, I found it hard to believe my bleary blood-shot eyes. He was ready for work. I searched for some sign that he'd been drinking all night and had only had four hours sleep. Nothing, the bastard. He sat at the kitchen table and proceeded to devour the cooked breakfast I could only poke with my fork. I was slowly coming to the conclusion that when it came to 'the gargle', I was way out of my league.

After Ciaran left, we drank several cups of tea and chatted with his mother and father. I gradually worked my way from liquids to solids.

Not surprisingly, our plans for the day were fairly vague. Eventually we took a bus into the city and just sort of wandered around. I was still feeling pretty downmarket by the time we found ourselves among the upmarket Georgian houses around Merrion Square. Every one of them had an elegance that shouted money and taste, the kind that always makes me think they're inhabited by people who write great novels, compose music, split atoms or find cures for the world's diseases, and don't go out all night getting rat-faced. Several of the houses had little information plaques beside their front doors, which explained how remarkably close I was to the mark. From where I was standing they had more than a hint of self-righteousness.

Next we wandered over to Grafton Street, the kind

of shopping strip I tend to avoid because no matter how much money you have, the beautiful objects beckoning from the immaculate shopfronts make you feel poor. As we looked in the windows, trying not to make eye contact with the shop assistants, I felt an odd affinity with the street beggars.

On the street corner opposite St Stephen's Green we noticed a theatre where Brendan Behan's *Borstal Boy* was playing.

'Behan. Is it any good?' Twidkiwodm asked.

I racked my brains, which really hurt. I vaguely remembered a movie version I'd seen, which I hadn't thought much of. Actually, it was crap, if I'm going to be entirely honest. But everyone in Ireland spoke of Behan with great reverence. So it was a toss-up: either I didn't have a clue, or the local boy was highly overrated. Rather than colour Twidkiwodm's opinion (and to neatly avoid appearing clueless) I played her enquiry with a straight bat. 'It's supposed to be,' I replied, ambiguously. Fortunately, just then the traffic lights changed and I drew her across the street to St Stephen's Green.

This is reputed to be one of Dublin's finest parks and it's also thought to be extremely old. No one knows exactly how old, but they can date the year they enclosed it with a fence: 1664. As parks go it's not particularly big, just a couple of hectares, although it has the usual park accoutrements such as statues of Irish heroes and writers, duck ponds, lakeside pavilions and benches.

'It's not looking good,' I concluded.

'What are you talking about?' Twidkiwodm disagreed. 'It's lovely.'

'Yes, but I've been looking everywhere and I haven't seen a single sign that says it's one of the greens.'

'Sorry?'

'Well, they're always saying Ireland has forty shades of green – light green, olive green, lime green. I just want to know if there's a St Stephen's Green? See that grass over there. If that was the official St Stephen's Green, I'd be really impressed.'

Twidkiwodm stopped and looked at me. 'You're still hung over, aren't you?'

'A bit.'

Not only was there no official St Stephen's Green, there was nowhere to buy lunch in the park, so we returned to Grafton Street and one of Dublin's best known nosh pits, Bewley's Oriental Café. While Twidkiwodm found a table, I found a list of the prices.

Alarm set in. All I could afford was coffee and a sandwich. Still, considering that was about all I could keep down, it wasn't so bad.

The coffee turned out to be quite good and the bacon, lettuce and tomato sandwich settled fairly gently on my somewhat delicate stomach. That is, until Twidkiwodm announced that she wanted to nip out and buy something she'd seen in Grafton Street. Suddenly, I didn't feel at all well. As far as I was concerned, any purchase in the immediate vicinity was fiscal recklessness. Matters didn't improve as the minutes passed and she didn't return. I started feeling queasy.

I was having hot flushes by the time the bill came. Then the table got cleared. I was asked if I wanted anything else. Even if I did, I couldn't afford it. I got up, paid and went out the front. More time passed.

I started wondering if something had happened. Perhaps Irish slave traders had leapt on Twidkiwodm from an alley. I could see a sack containing her unconscious form slumped in some rusty scow floating slowly down the Liffey. Then she was coming to in a harem, dressed only in…

'Why didn't you wait inside?' Twidkiwodm was at my side, interrupting my reverie. Damn it.

'They needed the table for a dinner reservation,' I replied, with more than a hint of sarcasm. 'Where the hell have you been?'

'Buying these,' she said, holding up two tickets. '*Borstal Boy*. Tonight.'

Oh God. If she wanted to surprise me, she'd succeeded. Now I was getting a first-hand lesson in why honesty is the best policy. It's cheaper.

'Fabulous,' I said. 'Thank you, darling.' I'll never learn. There was an upside, though. If we went out to a play, the boys couldn't take us drinking again.

IT WAS GETTING on and we decided that while we were in Dublin the one thing we still had to do was visit the Guinness brewery. It took quite a bit of getting to. A bus. Another bus. A lot of waiting. Finally, we were in the vicinity.

As we walked along, we were excited to find what looked like a slum. Up until then, Dublin had been disappointingly spick and span, unlike the literature-induced image we had of the struggling, hardship-enduring Irish. So seeing a block of flats in a dilapidated condition was a novelty, even if it wasn't terribly squalid. Curse that Celtic Tiger economy. Whatever happened to the underclass that inspired the line 'The Irish are the blacks of Europe' in Roddy Doyle's *The Commitments*?

We wondered if we were in the area someone in a pub had told us about, that had come up with a novel solution to the local drug problem. As the story went the community decided something had to be done about the dealers who hung around on the corners of the local park, openly selling drugs to children. The locals tried telling the dealers to leave, to no effect. So someone went to Northern Ireland to seek help from the IRA, who said that for a fee the problem would be solved. The locals took up a collection, paid the money and in due course a man from the IRA appeared at the park. He went around and told each drug dealer that they had half an hour to leave. When he came back, they were still there. So he went from corner to corner and shot them all.

Not far away, at St James's Gate, we suffered the kind of trauma only travellers can understand. The brewery's exhibition area and bar was about to shut! As we were planning to leave Dublin the next day and head off into the country, Guinness brewery day was today or never.

I blamed Brendan Behan. If Twidkiwodm hadn't taken so long over those tickets, we'd have had plenty of time for the brewery (there aren't many people who can say that Brendan Behan has come between them and a brewery). On the other hand, if we'd checked the guidebook we'd have known the exhibition closed early on Fridays. Not that I was going to admit as much as we went through the exhibits at a gallop. There was no time to read all the signs, so I gave a quick commentary on everything I knew about Guinness – how it's brewed; how Arthur Guinness started making his singular beverage in the eighteenth century based on the porter which originated in Covent Garden (where, yes, it was popular among porters); how in 1759 Guinness signed a 9,000-year lease on the St James's Gate Brewery…

'Wait a second,' Twidkiwodm interrupted. 'If you already knew all this, why did we have to come here?'

'Because there's more, much more.'

Twidkiwodm gave me an odd look.

'There's free Guinness,' I sheepishly confessed.

'I thought so,' was all she said.

As we continued rapidly through the rooms, I assumed the reason they were deserted was that the place was about to close. Then we got to the bar area.

It was packed.

When I say 'free Guinness', I mean that after you've paid the brewery entry fee they give you a token for a free pint at the Guinness bar, hereafter known as The Source. Of course, it's one of those laws of human nature that you're going to use that token whether you like Guinness or not. Thus all the tables and chairs were occupied by people you wouldn't normally pick as Guinness drinkers: Japanese tour groups, young Italian couples, little old ladies. Everyone was chugging pints. For many of them, it was obviously their first taste. And because Guinness is an acquired taste, the expressions on a lot of the faces were alone worth the price of admission.

So what was Guinness at The Source like? One thing was immediately obvious: it was fresh. This is particularly interesting given that every day in Ireland they consume around two million pints of the stuff. In other words, stale Guinness is pretty much an oxymoron. I recalled what Willie Simpson, a beer writer of my acquaintance, once wrote about where one should drink beer: it's generally best when you're within sight of the brewery. Freshness was part of it but in the case of Guinness he added that in Dublin the beer isn't pasteurised because it's consumed as quickly as it's produced. So it should taste the same all across town. And what about Dinger's claim that the best Guinness was sent to the west? There was only one way to find out.

AFTER THE BAR closed we wandered around outside for a while. We took photos of the cobbled street leading to the big black gate with the word Guinness picked out in gold, which features in a lot of the Guinness posters. Up the centre of the street there were tracks for a miniature railway line and I imagined little Guinness trains chuffing out of the brewery en route to stations with exotic names like Liverish, Inebrious and Throbbinghead.

We decided shanks's pony could get us back to town faster than the buses, so we strolled over to the Liffey and followed it downstream. Along the way I bought a copy of *The Essential James Joyce* in a small bookshop. Then we found a small pub, which we entered to have a Guinness. As we spread our maps and book on the table, the locals looked at us suspiciously. Or perhaps that story about drug dealers was really about tourists.

Back in the city, we bumped into Katrin. Again. She was still very beautiful, perhaps having returned to her hostel far earlier than we had retired the night before. We started explaining what we'd done since we'd last seen each other. Or rather, I did.

Twidkiwodm was standing at my side, strangely silent. As the conversation continued, there was a coolness in the air that was unmistakable.

'And what do you do tonight?' Katrin enquired.

'We have tickets to a play,' stated Twidkiwodm, with a pretty obvious subtext. It may even have been in German.

'Which one?'

'*Borstal Boy*. Brendan Behan.'

'I've heard of him. He was very famous.'

'Yes. I think the play is sold out.'

The three of us strolled towards the Ha'penny Bridge, chatting as we went. Eventually, we went our separate ways.

'What an amazing coincidence. Again,' I said, trying to keep it light.

'I think she's stalking us.'

'Really?' I replied. I'd always wanted to be stalked by a ravishing Teutonic beauty. Actually, that's not true. But now that I was, it seemed a pretty good ambition.

I should perhaps mention that Twidkiwodm also

has some German heritage. Not that the connection was particularly big. About the only way it manifested itself was in a fairly strong will. That and being tall and blond, with steely blue eyes – which were fixed on me at that moment with more steeliness than usual.

BACK IN TOWN we met up with Ciaran after he finished work and told him our plans for the evening.

'Behan? He's controvorsial,' he said. 'The language is fookin' strong. And there's noodity.'

That didn't sound at all like the movie version. Things were looking up.

'*Borstal Boy* is it?' his mother said when we got home. 'Sure there's a lot of language but it's a fine piece.'

Under the circumstances I erred on the diplomatic side regarding my expectations for the evening's entertainment. And I was starting to wonder what that film had done to *Borstal Boy* to make it so bad.

After an early feast, Ciaran drove us across town and pointed out a pub where he'd meet us for a pint after the show. At least now I had something to look forward to. After he dropped us at the theatre, we went in, bought a programme and found our seats, some more reluctantly than others. And then, to my absolute surprise, the curtain rose and I was immediately enthralled.

The play was shiveringly good. If you don't know much about Irish politics, and I readily confess that before I'd set foot in Ireland I thought I did but I really didn't, then you could do worse than see *Borstal Boy*. Is it political? It's 'fookin' political'. But it makes you realise that what happened 100 years or even 300 years ago is still affecting the quality of life people have today. By the end of it, I actually felt like I understood what was at stake in Ireland, from both sides.

We were buzzing with excitement when we found Ciaran in Neery's, the pub where we'd arranged to meet. Naturally, we ordered pints of Guinness. Better than the pint at the brewery? Yes. But I suspect that a good pint in a fine Dublin pub after seeing a great Irish play has a taste all its own.

While we came down from the performance, Ciaran told us he'd grown up in the same neighbourhood as Behan. 'But I'm not into books very mooch. I only really know the Oirish wroiters we stoodied in school. And there's a few wroiters' festivals oi've hoard of.' He then gave us a comprehensive rundown of both.

After we left Neery's, he took us to try and find

the house of *Dracula* author, Bram Stoker. I doubt there are many countries where telephone engineers could take you on an impromptu literary tour after delivering a dissertation on their nation's writers. But maybe literature is so integrated into Dublin's cultural fabric that it springs to the surface in nearly everyone.

We poked around in the dark until we found Bram's place. It wasn't particularly scary, just one of a row of elegant terraces with nary a cobweb, bat or hideous spectre of the undead to be seen. But thus reassured that the streets were safe, we tackled the long walk back to Ciaran's house (he'd left his car at home since he was going to a pub). As we walked, Ciaran told us that the estate where his mother lived had formerly been owned by the Catholic Church. 'On Sondays the priests used to go around making sure their tenants went to mass,' he said. 'If dey didn't go, dey soomtoims found themselves out on the street.'

It sounded like a case of the landlord moving in mysterious ways.

WHEN IT CAME to the timing of our arrival in Ireland, it turned out we'd managed to be in exactly the right place at the right time (with some dispute from our livers, which were wishing they were anywhere but here) because our first weekend was a bank holiday. The boys had already planned a trip to Killarney, on the west coast, and although Ciaran's car was already full we were invited.

The west coast. Aka Guinness Mecca.

On Saturday morning Ciaran picked up his girlfriend Winnie, Pat, and a couple of mates, and headed off. Ciaran's father drove us to the bus station, from where we'd head for Tralee, just up the road from Killarney. The boys were going to nab us some accommodation at a hostel when they got there. All we had to do was find it, check in and then meet them at one of their favourite pubs. Bet you never saw that coming.

Ciaran's father seemed to feel compelled to make conversation and gradually warmed to the subject of his days in law enforcement. When he pulled up outside the bus station, he just kept talking. The gist was that while wholesale violence wasn't permitted in the Garda, there were times when ill-behaved citizens needed 'a little persuading'. Once the car was stopped and he had free use of his hands, he explained at length the ways in which this could be done. Soon we were armed with enough knowledge of unarmed combat that we could have had our extremities registered as lethal weapons. Then, because we were hoping to go to areas where Gaelic was spoken, he also insisted on giving us some phrases he thought would be useful. We paid close attention, but apparently this wasn't enough. He made us write them down.

Sláinte go saol agat meant 'Health and good life to you'. The short form, 'Cheers', was simply *Sláinte*. *Go raibh maith agat* was 'Thank you'. *Slán agat* was 'Goodbye'.

I saw my chance. 'I'm afraid we're going to have to say *slán agat*. We've got to buy our bus tickets,' I said, hoping this would buy our freedom.

'Oh yes. I'm sorry, I have been going on,' he said.

'So,' I said firmly as I finally managed to get the car door open. '*Go raibh maith agat* for the lift into town. And *slán agat*.' I shook his hand.

'*Slán agat*,' he said. 'And you won't be forgetting the toast.'

'No, no,' I said, as Twidkiwodm and I extracted ourselves from the car in a process not unlike removing teeth. Finally, we shut the door and he drove off. When he was out of sight we turned to the entrance doors of the bus station. And there was

Katrin. Still beautiful. And yet, slightly creepy.

It turned out she was heading out of town on a bus as well. We enquired which direction she was heading in.

'North,' she said. 'I am wanting to go to a festival of music.'

'We're heading to the west coast,' Twidkiwodm explained. But I could detect a sense of relief that reminded me of Hemingway's story, 'The Light of the World', in which one of the characters, when asked which way he was going, replied 'The other way from you.'

4

BLOOD IS THICKER
THAN GUINNESS

When Russians want to tempt fate, they play
Russian roulette. And let's face it, playing with
firearms is the sort of thing you'd find yourself doing
if you lived in a place where the weather report for
six months of the year read, 'Blizzard with an 80 per
cent chance of death from exposure'. With Russian
roulette there's usually a one in six chance you'll be
in the wrong place at the wrong time.

When the Irish want to tempt fate, they play Irish
roulette. No firearms involved – they just go for a
drive. On the bus ride to Tralee we got a taste of
what it's like. Basically, the traffic in each direction

had a lane each, with a sort of edge you could pull onto in an emergency or while being passed. If someone pulled over for you, you could use your own lane to overtake. Or you could use the oncoming lane while the cars there pulled over. How do you know when it's safe to do that? I never worked it out.

You hear stories of Irish people who never travel beyond their own valley. After your first experience of Irish roads, you begin to understand why. Matters aren't helped by the logo of the national bus company, Bus Éireann. It includes a picture of an Irish setter running along at full pelt. Setters are generally regarded as friendly and loyal but also as not very bright and highly erratic. So it isn't clear just what kind of message Bus Éireann is trying to send. It doesn't get any better if you look closely at the dog. I swear it has its eyes firmly shut.

The road system and this image playing on my mind did not make for a relaxing journey. The other passengers didn't help either. While the bus demonstrated that in Ireland there's no such thing as a short distance between two points, the people behind us set about driving us mad by playing Abba over and over on their walkpersons. If I'd entertained any thoughts of penning reveries regarding the passing Irish countryside, they met their Waterloo at the hands of Fernando. We sat through hours of disco torment Joyce could have added to his scenes from hell.

WHEN AT LAST we got to Tralee, we found a neat and tidy regional centre with several nice parks, brightly painted shopfronts, and houses set in well-kept gardens. In a word: disappointing. Not that it was Tralee's fault. It's just that 'The Rose of Tralee', which throughout childhood we were doomed to learn on the recorder, had rather raised our expectations. I was expecting streets that thronged with rose-like girls. On the Saturday afternoon of a bank holiday weekend, there was a marked absence of girls generally and ones of rose-like complexion in particular.

The town does have a Rose of Tralee festival, every year in August, but if you miss it all those recorder lessons will have been for nought. What the place needs is a flying squad of comely lasses who stand on selected corners year round – at least on weekends – swishing their flowing dresses back and forth, maybe even handing out roses to passing tourists.

Twidkiwodm refused to impersonate one, even for a photo. Instead, she hustled in the direction of the road to Killarney.

THE DAY WAS getting on and we still had to hitchhike about thirty kilometres. We stopped just past a petrol station we planned to retreat to if it started to rain, which it was threatening to do. Although there were still several hours of daylight left, it was growing darker by the minute as the clouds piled in.

A car came along and we got ready with our thumbs. It pulled into the petrol station, and a woman got out and started filling her car. We could see she had a couple of children with her, so even if she was heading our way we could count her out. But no, the woman came back, got into her car and drove over to us.

'I can take you as far as Killarney,' she said.

Our jaws dropped. 'Are you sure?'

'It's no trooble at all,' she replied. 'Hop in.'

Welcome to the west coast. It's the only place I've been where a woman with kids would pick up hitchhikers. And she even made one of the kids hop in the back, so one of us could have the front seat. Our first ride and we hadn't even stuck out our thumbs.

As we headed down the road I couldn't help commenting on how 'unlikely' it was to be picked up by a mum and her kids. She took the subtext 'Are you out of your mind?' quite well.

'Oh no,' she said. 'I looked you over at the petrol station. I could tell you were nice people. Australians, do you say?'

It started to rain. We felt grateful for the comfort of the car as we passed people hitchhiking at farm gates, presumably heading into Killarney for a big Saturday night out. It was while we drove that my chance for a reverie about the Irish countryside arrived. Dark-grey clouds were hanging low over the gently sloping green hills. In the gloom the wet green grass was almost luminous. The fields were enclosed by moss-covered rock walls that were dark with moisture, light with lichen.

Fortunately for all concerned, the woman interrupted my reverie to tell us the rain was much needed. 'It's been quite droi. Well, droi by our standards. I believe it's very droi in Australia.'

'Our farmers would kill for grass this green,' I replied.

'Is that roit now? Well our forty shades of green are what we're famous for but roit now yer not seein' the coontry at its best.'

I thought it looked terrific. And seeing as she'd brought up the forty shades, there was something I wanted to ask her, but a sense of imminent danger emanating from the back seat kept me quiet.

KILLARNEY WAS PACKED. When we eventually found the boys in a pub called The Laurels, it seemed that most of Ireland had decided to join them. In fact, the place was filled with people from around the world. It looked like a league of beer- and stout-drinking nations engaged in a dialogue that was in essence a roar.

We met Ciaran's 'mot', Winnie, a slender dark-haired woman with a ready smile, and Ciaran's and Pat's mates, one of whom was an interesting-looking character named Gerry. He looked as if his five o'clock shadow grew in about half an hour after he shaved, say by 8.30 in the morning. He had such a wild desperado air that I felt he'd be holding up the bar just before closing, but his nature was the opposite of the way he looked.

Gerry and the others were talking to three girls they'd met earlier in the afternoon. When they introduced us we knew we'd have no trouble remembering their names. All three were called Sheila. They were all locals, all close friends, and all proof that Killarney needs a new book of baby names.

We battled to the bar, waited for the Guinness to be poured and when we had a couple of pints in our hands settled down to enjoy an atmosphere as typical of an Irish pub as you could expect – even though the Irish were outnumbered at least two to one. There was another slight difference, too. A sign over the bar read 'No singin''.

'What have they got against singing?' I asked one of the Sheilas.

'Oh, they've a place for singin' out the back. For the tourists. They don't like anywoon singin' in here because it gets too congested.'

Surveying the sardine-like arrangements currently operating in the front bar, one could only guess at how they could tell the difference.

Still The Laurels was as good a place as any to consider the question of whether the Guinness was better in the west than it was in Dublin. It was very good. But to be honest, it tasted neither better nor worse than the pints we'd sampled anywhere else. Not that we minded – it just meant our work was far from done.

During the evening, though, some bloke who'd opened a conversation with the standard line 'I see you're drinkin' the Guinness' ventured the opinion that the Guinness is better in Dublin. 'It doosn't travel well,' the man told me. 'All that bouncing on the trooks doos it no good at all. And the Doobliners are a foosy boonch. They couldn't serve shite to them dere. Dere'd be a roi-it.'

You may recall I'd been told something similar about the west coast while I was in Dublin, but I thought better of pointing this out. Personally, on first impressions, and perhaps excluding Neery's after *Borstal Boy* and the Guinness brewery bar, I'd have called it a tie. I headed to the bar to do some more research.

We learned quite a few other things during the course of the evening. Such as: 'If you're looky, you'll be foinding the poteen.' It seemed we were in the heart of the poteen country. A guy told us there were illegal stills hidden all over the place in the wild hills around the Killarney Lakes. We also learned that the Irish are as friendly in the country as they are in the city. Everyone was ready for a chat, which is just as well as I sometimes come over all shy when I'm talking to strangers. In The Laurels it was hard to get even a monosyllable in.

Typically, you might say, we stayed until they threw us out. This took some doing because by closing time nearly the entire pub had become close friends and it was a question of moving the craic elsewhere. After buying every bottle and can the place could muster, the customers spilled out into the street. It was like walking into a carnival. All the pubs were closing and hundreds of fairly intoxicated people were milling around the town. This sort of thing might seriously alarm most police forces, but in Killarney all we saw was one Garda car parked in the main square while the officers gave directions to disoriented visitors. Some of them were as disoriented as newts.

One of the more interesting spectacles was the numerous couples engaged in intimate communion in every nook and cranny of the town. They may have been good Catholic boys and girls, but we're not talking holy communion. There didn't appear to be any actual sex but what I witnessed made me wonder whether children with names like Marguerite, Violet and Rose were named after the beds of flowers they'd been conceived in.

We sat in the square drinking for a while until the cold and rain drove us indoors. We were also getting concerned that we would be locked out of the hostel if we left it much longer. So we decided to smuggle our drinks into the hostel kitchen and finish them there, despite a sign that said alcohol couldn't be consumed on the premises.

We got in without any trouble and headed for the kitchen. It was dark, the coast seemed clear, so we turned on the… d'oh! Sitting by the window was the hostel manager. We apologised and switched out the light, hoping darkness would conceal the suspicious bag we were carrying and the party of half a dozen that was accompanying us.

'Coom in, coom in,' he called across the room. 'Don't moind me. Torn on the loit.'

Fortunately, I was quick with an excuse. 'I hope you don't mind,' I said. 'We've just got a few beers we wanted to finish before we went to bed.'

The others looked at me. OK, it wasn't much of an excuse. More like a confession really.

'No, you're foin,' the man said. 'Coom and sit down. We only make dat rool about drinkin' to stop the place tornin' into a madhouse.'

Maybe honesty really is the best policy.

We moved towards the table he was sitting at and it was then that I noticed he was drinking something from a lemonade bottle. It was a clear liquid but didn't appear to have the bubbles you usually associate with lemonade. I sat down and remarked, 'Would I be right in assuming that what's in that bottle isn't actually lemonade?'

'You would,' he said. 'It's what we call poteen. And if you give me soom of dat beer, oil let you troi soom.'

So as it turned out, finding the poteen wasn't that hard to do. We started organising glasses. However, before I tasted the illegal distilment, there was something I had to ask.

'Why were you sitting here in the dark?' I said to the manager. If an aversion to light, inability to sleep or ending up mad as a cut snake was a consequence of drinking poteen, I wanted to know beforehand.

'I was keepin' an oi on a guest's motorbike outsoid,' he said. 'There's so many people out tonight I taught it better to be on the safe soid.'

The manager was just as generous with the poteen. It was as clear as water, but the similarities ended there. One whiff was enough. Wine is often described as having a bouquet; beer has what they call an aroma. Poteen? This stuff gave off fumes – of alcohol and not much else. As for the taste, for a moment I was back on the ferry crossing to Dun Laoghaire, having a Proustian recollection of flavours past. But the poteen had a lot more bite than Guinness. Actually it had more bite than a Bengal tiger. I couldn't blame the hostel manager for wanting our beer.

I rolled the poteen around for a moment and quickly found myself smiling because when it hit my cheeks they tightened so much that the sides of my mouth were pulled back involuntarily. It didn't so much have a flavour as an impact. It was the kind of thing which, if you'd drunk it when you were a kid, you'd think, 'Nope, better not have any more of this. Better take the bottle to Mum and see if I need to go to hospital.'

Being an adult, I emptied the glass instead. It was strong, but not lethally so – at least as it went down. Maybe later, things would be different. I wasn't surprised when everyone refused a second glass. They joined the manager in finishing off the beer. By the time we crept to bed, we still weren't feeling any after-effects. That is, unless dreaming of stomach pumps all night counts as an after-effect.

SUNDAY MORNING DAWNED with a blue sky and church bells. And compared to the night before, the streets were almost deserted. Here and there a few old

American couples waddled along the footpaths in bulging leisure suits, looking lost. Perhaps they don't have good guidebooks in America, because American tourists spend most of their time saying 'Or you shrrr it's this way'. But at least these Americans go and explore other parts of the world. I salute their struggle. The Americans I worry about are the ones who stay at home, insulated and brooding.

Twidkiwodm and I spent the morning exploring the town. Despite the pressures of tourism it was a pleasant place, especially when it was quiet. About the only thing that distinguished it from a town like Tralee was that there seemed to be a lot more signs, many of which pointed the way to the nearby lakes. The lakes were a little way out of town, but fortified with a breakfast of fried eggs, bacon and toast we headed out on foot. We were constantly passed by horse-drawn carts full of Americans. They looked happier than the ones we'd seen in town, perhaps because being driven around solved the problem of which way they were going. Only a few – New Yorkers, I assume – looked worried, presumably because the carts didn't have meters they could watch.

The road ended at a carpark on the edge of Lough Leane. It must be hard being a famous lake. One day you're minding your own business, lapping your shores. The next there are all these cruise boats motoring up and down with commentaries explaining why you're so special. Soon you find yourself worrying how your scenery looks. Are those clouds making the light shift the right way? Are your waters crystal-clear enough? No wonder the Killarney Lakes are renowned for having changing moods.

The day we saw it, Lough Leane's mood was best described as taciturn. A stiff breeze had kicked up a nasty little chop that was smacking and spraying on the rocky shore, making the lake less than inviting. As for the mountains that were supposed to be wild and ruggedly beautiful, they looked more like they'd had too much sun and were soaking their feet in the lake to cool off.

Near the carpark stood the ruined fifteenth-century Ross Castle. Oliver Cromwell did the ruining in 1653. A sign said the castle had been the last stronghold of the Irish, but it's unlikely it could have withstood the tourist hordes either. Most of them were snapping the ruins and then heading for the docks where the tour boats were bobbing on the lake. Rather than add to its burden and deplete our finances further, we found a short walk that would take us along the water's edge and only cost a little shoe leather. Within moments we were swallowed by the scenery: the sounds of traffic and people faded as the path wound away around the edge of the lake and its deeply forested shores.

From time to time a boat would putt past and a snatch of commentary could be heard from the loudspeakers telling the passengers things like 'Walking is a popular pastime around our beautiful lakes'. Obviously not as popular as sitting on your bum being told about it, though, as for an hour we had the path and the lake almost to ourselves.

At one spot the path wound through a forest carpeted with sphagnum moss and illumined by shafts of sunlight. Beyond the trees, we could glimpse the water sparkling in the distance. It wasn't hard to imagine it as a place where mythical creatures – fairies or leprechauns – held their rituals. Even if they didn't exist, this was the kind of place that inspired you to create them.

Back at the carpark the tourist groups were still taking snaps. In many cases the film in their cameras was probably exposed to the view for longer than they were. They didn't know what they were missing. At least walking gives you a bit of time for contemplation. Even better is stopping, even if it's just for a minute or two. Hey, go crazy – spend five minutes. The advantage of being still is that all the things which hid when you came along relax and come out again. And the longer you look, the more you see.

I've since found out (from my Australian editor) that there's actually a word for this type of walk. She called it a ramble.

ON THE ROAD back to town we found a hostel we liked the look of and after checking it out we booked in for the following night. Such spontaneity is one of the advantages of travelling without a clear plan. The disadvantage is that at other times you can end up sleeping in a manger.

Back in town we made our way to The Laurels for lunch and to quench our 'terrible torst' after all that walking. Compared to the night before the place was practically deserted. We ordered our Guinnesses and sat down to wait while they were poured. We got chatting to a girl from Cork, named Kate, who was also in town for the weekend. Our half-poured drinks sat on the bar until we started to wonder if the barman was ever going to come back. By the time he returned we knew most of Kate's life story. Finally, I went over and got the beers.

I also ordered another round, anticipating that they would be ready about the time we finished the first ones. I wasn't wrong. When they were poured the barman just sat them on the counter and disappeared down to the back bar. When he returned, I went over to pay.

'Yes sorr,' the barman said. 'What can I get you?'

'I'd like to pay.'

'Pay? What for?'

'You poured us a couple of Guinnesses about five minutes ago.'

'Did I? Are you sure?'

It was the first time I'd seen a barman not only forget that he'd served you but that he hadn't charged you either. Only in Ireland on a slow Sunday afternoon.

LIKE MOST TOWNS that are tourist centres, Killarney was tidal. In the morning the tourists poured out to the surrounding attractions. At dusk they came flooding back, filling the streets, the pubs, the restaurants.

Conscious that the tide was about to come in, we left The Laurels in search of dinner. We could have stayed and had some pub grub, but we thought we'd broaden our horizons. By the time we got back, the place was packed. Considering we'd only been in Killarney a day we were surprised how many people we knew – Ciaran, Winnie, Patrick, their mates, the Sheilas. The crowd was big, noisy and friendly. At one point someone broke the 'No singin'' rule and started on a Beatles song. The entire pub joined in, sang it all the way through, then stopped. Just the one song, after which it was back to talking and drinking.

During the night I had another 'If yer looky, ye moit be foindin' the poteen' conversation, but this time I could say I'd already succeeded, just the night before.

'Oh now,' the man said, clearly shocked. 'You want to be careful around that stoof.'

I was surprised by his sudden change of tack, not to mention the possibility that we'd just done something really stupid (again).

'If yer not careful, it'll send ye blind.'

'Blind drunk?' I asked hopefully.

He shook his head.

Well, there wasn't much I could do about it now. While I still had my vision I asked, 'Whose shout is it anyway?' not wanting to lose sight of what really mattered.

MAYBE IT'S JUST me, but I suspect that most men dream of having women fight over them. In The Laurels, that dream was nearly fulfilled. It happened when I was sitting at a table with the three Sheilas and their friends. It was pretty lively, with several conversations going on at once, and at one point one of the girls tried to attract another's attention. The other girl was so focused on what someone else was saying that she didn't notice, so the first girl dipped her fingers in some Guinness and flicked it at her. Girl Two got splashed, turned to Girl One and took it the wrong way. She dipped her fingers in her Guinness and splashed her back. Girl One got more than she bargained for, soaked her fingers in Guinness and gave Girl Two plenty. At which point both girls picked up their glasses and threw them at each other.

Fortunately for them, the glasses met in mid-air and smashed to pieces. Guinness and broken glass rained onto the table. Unfortunately for Boy One (me), my hand was resting on exactly that part of the table and a large chunk of glass landed on it. The broken glass, creamy froth and black Guinness were immediately joined by a new substance. It was red and there was plenty of it. To assess the damage, I poured my pint over my hand to wash away the debris. One look was all I needed.

'Where's the nearest hospital?' I said. 'And would someone go and get Michelle?'

While one of the Sheilas started organising transportation, the management contributed a bar towel to staunch the blood. But there was still no Twidkiwodm. 'Did someone tell her what's happened?'

'She doesn't believe it,' one of the Sheilas replied. 'She said it was a nice try but she's not going to stop talking to the fella she's with.'

Feeling a bit like the boy who cried wolf I peered through the smoke to where Twidkiwodm was 'mingling'. When I managed to catch her eye I held up a hand wrapped in a blood-soaked towel. She looked shocked for a moment, then turned to the bloke (who looked pretty damn lupine himself) and presumably explained to him that she had to take her boyfriend to hospital. I would have loved to hear that particular conversation.

Not surprisingly for 10 o'clock on a Sunday night, the hospital was dark in the kind of dark way that only places which are shut can be.

'It looks shut,' someone said.

'No, there'll be soomwoon dere,' said the Sheila who'd driven. She went up to the front door and pounded on it as hard as she could. Faintly at first, there was a sound of unhurried footsteps at the end of a very long corridor. Eventually, the door opened a crack.

'We've a lad here who's cot himself,' Sheila said. 'He's needin' medical attention.'

I pushed my hand towards the light.

'Oh yes,' a woman said, surveying my gaping wound. 'I'd say dat moit take a stitch or two. The doctor's joost leavin'. Coom in and I'll see if we can catch him.'

We were ushered into a foyer and left there while a search ensued. Five minutes later the nurse returned. 'You're in look,' she said. 'He was just gettin' into his car when we found him.'

She ushered our little band along corridor after corridor until we arrived in what looked disturbingly like an operating theatre. The doctor was a middle-aged man in a tweed jacket with wisps of hair floating out of control around his head.

'Now den, what have ye doon t'yerself?'

Although I had no reason to doubt his medical skills, his thick Irish brogue late at night in a hospital surgery was a little disconcerting. Fighting the urge to run, I told him how I'd got my wound. I suspect he only pretended to believe me.

'Australian are ye? Well, I'd say you'll be havin' a permanent souvenir to remember oos by.'

He got himself organised, cleaned the wound and started putting in the first stitch, without anaesthetic.

'Doctor,' Sheila piped up. 'Don't you think you should be givin' him soomthin' for the pain?'

The doctor didn't look up. He just said, 'I don't think he's feelin' any pain.'

He might have been right, but making jokes at his patient's expense didn't seem much of a bedside manner. At least his jibes took my mind off the stitches – all two of them.

When the doctor was finished, he bandaged me up and gave me a tube of antiseptic cream. 'Put that on woonce a day. The stitches should coom out in a week.'

I said thanks and asked how much.

'No need to woory about dat,' he said. 'Enjoy your holiday and troi to stay out of trooble.'

BACK IN TOWN, the craic had moved on to a local disco. It was getting late and the sensible thing to do was to go to bed. On the other hand – as in, the one that had the stitches in it – you can get loads of attention from people who are concerned about your welfare after you've been heavily bandaged, post bloody injury, and you appear to be in excruciating pain. At the disco I was surrounded by girls intent on soothing and comforting.

The bloke who had been chatting up Twidkiwodm was at the disco, too, but for some reason the chemistry was no longer there. She spent half an hour watching me milk my sore paw for all it was worth before telling me that I was making her nauseous and we had to leave.

LOVE AT FIRST PINT

The next day, due to my extensive injuries, we put off going on a tour of the famous Ring of Kerry and moved our base to the hostel on the Lough Leane road. It was a lovely old building in well-tended grounds, and we discovered, on checking in, that it had a rowboat that guests could take out on the lake.

Monday was the last day of the holiday weekend and also Ciaran and Pat's last day with us, so we had farewell drinks – where else but at The Laurels. It was there that we saw Gerry fall in love.

A girl came over and asked if anyone was sitting

in one of the empty chairs. Gerry replied with the usual 'Yes. You are.'

The two of them started talking. Among the angels that pass for women in Ireland, this girl was something special. She wasn't just pretty, she was sweetness and sunshine made flesh and blood. The contrast with the blue-chinned, desperate-looking Gerry could not have been more striking. No one paid them much attention, but after a while we couldn't help noticing their heads move closer. They seemed to be discussing items of more than just general interest. A little more time and they were holding hands and murmuring to each other. Their cheeks brushed. They exchanged a kiss.

All this took place while Pat, Ciaran, Winnie, Twidkiwodm, two of the Sheilas and a few other people sat around them drinking, exchanging stories and telling jokes. Next time we looked, they were kissing in earnest and wrapped in each other's arms. In an hour and a half they'd gone from complete strangers to soul mates. And it wasn't just a passing passion. It was obvious to all of us that these two had found each other. It was as romantic as all get out. At the rate they were going he'd have proposed by sunset.

It was then that disaster struck. The girl realised that her train was leaving in half an hour. Gerry was from Dublin. She was from Cork. The weekend was over and she had to leave. A desperate scene ensued. People started ringing the station to see if there was a later train. The last one was an hour later, so they booked her on that. The boys said they'd drive her and Gerry to the station so they could spend as much time together as possible before they were cruelly torn apart. (This even though they'd exchanged phone numbers and addresses and arranged to meet in Cork the next weekend.)

Twidkiwodm and I had to miss the final farewell at the station because there wasn't enough room in the car and from there the boys were heading straight on to Dublin. Before they left The Laurels we said our own goodbyes, little knowing it would be years before we saw Pat and Ciaran again. And Gerry and the girl? I don't know what happened to them. Maybe they're married and living happily ever after.

BACK AT OUR new accommodation we decided a sunset row on the lake would cap the day nicely. The hostel manager walked with us to the lake to make sure we found the boat OK. 'People soomtoims have trooble foindin' the roit woon,' he said. 'I'd hate for ye to have to come all the way back.'

We were walking along, chatting and enjoying the evening, when a voice started shouting at us from behind. We turned around to see what the commotion was about only to be confronted with the sight of a huge man running towards us in full Scottish regalia – kilt, sporran, socks, garters, shirt and tie. To complete the picture he had flaming red hair and a full red beard. We were a bit surprised. An enormous Scottish Highlander was about the last thing you'd expect to meet in a quiet Irish lane.

But we were wrong. 'Ze boot. Vill you be long viz it rowing?'

There was no doubt about it. He was German.

'I beg your pardon,' I said, mainly to hear him speak again so I could be sure about the accent.

'Ze boot. I vould like to be using zis when you are returning.' Yep. Definitely German.

'Why are you dressed like that?' I had to ask.

'I am boosker. I am finishing making music viz ze bagpipes for today and would like rowing on ze beautiful lakes.'

A German bagpipe player. That explained everything.

'Actually, we don't mind if you come with us,' I replied, 'but on one condition.'

'Zis is gut. But vot condition?'

'Bring the bagpipes.'

His face cracked into a huge grin. 'Ja. Very gut. You go boot. I catch you up.'

He bounded off back towards the hostel, kilt, beard and hair flying – rather like the dog in the Bus Éireann logo – and he almost beat us to the rowboat, which was one of those classic wooden numbers – long and narrow, with several benches set across it. As I was manually challenged, Twidkiwodm and I sat in the middle and shared the rowing, with an oar each. Our companion, who told us his name was Helge, sat in the stern constructing his bagpipes.

'All over Ireland I am boosking,' he said in answer to our questions. 'Making bagpipes music. Ze people are sinking I am from Scotland. They are giving me lots of money. Lots of beer.'

'Have you played in Scotland?' Twidkiwodm asked as we rowed out onto the lake.

'No,' he replied. 'I am not going in Scotland. For zis reason. In Scotland, ze kilt is make by special way. You know zis sings – pleats. Zis pleats I am learning is very expensive. But for making bagpipe music I am needing to look like zis kilt. Zo I am making from fabric not zo much. This fabric, in Scotland, is making for voman's dress. But is cheap. Ja?'

'You're wearing a dress?'

'In Scotland, I am sinking zey vill know zis. And zis is making zum peeple very angry. Could be zese peeple vill be making trouble. Zey may be kicking ze shit out of me.' From the size of him I didn't think he'd have much to worry about but you never know. He might well drive the Scots crazy.

It was when Helge had got his bagpipes organised that things got really interesting. When he was ready to play he did what every bagpipe player does. He stood up. Of course, he didn't tell us he was going to do it. We were taken unawares and the boat started rocking wildly, but Helge didn't bat an eyelid. He just started blowing and pumping up his bagpipes. While we tried to keep balance, he started to play.

This is how, one August evening on the famous Lakes of Killarney, a handful of small tour boats witnessed a sight probably never seen before or since. In the setting sun, a rowboat cut across the still Irish waters while the lone figure of a giant red-bearded German bagpiper (in a woman's dress) stood in the stern playing reels. All the little tour boats within earshot changed course to confirm that they really were seeing what they thought they were seeing. Every one of them was leaning dangerously as people crowded to the side to look.

Whenever a boat came near enough Helge broke off to yell across the water at them. 'Beer. Give us beer. Ve vant more beer.'

When he finally tired of creating general mayhem in the stern, Helge sat down and put the bagpipes away. Then he insisted on rowing. With more rocking of the boat we changed places, then Helge wrapped his enormous mitts around the oars and with a mighty heave that all but snapped them he launched the boat forward. His stroke rate could have won an Olympic medal (possibly in waterskiing).

'In Chermany I am making much rowing,' he told us as we passed the tour boats. Disconcertingly, his exertions didn't seem to be leaving him short of breath. 'I am taking my boot into ze North Zee many kilometres. Ze ocean is making many waves but I am enjoying zis type off rowing.'

There's a word for that kind of behaviour: Viking.

Oh, and one other thing we discovered. The bagpipes were made in Pakistan.

NOT ALL GERMANS are mad. That night we met two very sane ones at the hostel; Horst and Michael. Horst was short, dark and stocky, with a huge handlebar moustache. He was very much a man of the land. His family owned a vineyard in a mountainous part of Germany and it seemed that he spent most of his life in the role of mountain goat, tending the vines on the steep slopes.

Michael was tall and had an air of culture about him. They didn't seem to have a lot in common but it turned out the two of them had been friends since childhood.

They had always wanted to visit Ireland but they couldn't tell us why. They were fascinated by our adventures on the lake and, I suspect they were impressed by my wound.

From them we learned that there are two kinds of traveller in Ireland: clockwise and anticlockwise. Basically, everyone circumnavigates the place, going around the outside in one direction or the other. As it happened, we were going in the same direction they were – clockwise. Did it matter? Did it matter whether Jonathan Swift's Lilliputians opened their eggs at the pointy end or the round one?

We found out the next morning. When we started

on our tour of the Ring of Kerry, we discovered that we had unwittingly joined a tour that was going on a sixty seat coach, and that most of the passengers seemed to be disoriented Americans in leisure suits. When the driver told us that the coach was going to traverse the Ring anticlockwise, we started to suspect it wasn't a good sign.

However, we had no choice in the matter. All the big coaches had a convention whereby they all went around the Ring in an anticlockwise direction because the road is often too narrow for them to pass each other if they meet head on. We also had little choice in our mode of transport because it's 180 kilometres around the Ring and it would have taken us days to hitchhike. So we planned to go on the tour, check out the whole area, then if there were places we particularly liked, we'd go back there.

For the first part of the trip, hitchhiking would have been quicker. Getting out of Killarney took 40 minutes and it's not that big a town. It would be wrong to say the traffic moved at a crawl. Anything crawling would have beaten us out of Killarney easily.

The coach driver was a small Puckish-looking Irishman who kept up an entertaining banter as we edged along, endearing himself to most of his passengers instantly. He suggested the traffic jam was probably because 'We Irish don't park our cars. We abandon them.' He maintained his jovial demeanour until he finally came upon the cause of the delay – a delivery van. It was blocking one lane of the road leaving town, while its owner stood chatting to a shopkeeper and cars struggled to get around it. Presumably the conversation had been going on for close to an hour.

Our coach driver blew his horn. He was greeted with a casual wave. We rather expected the situation to be whimsically brushed aside as an example of idiosyncratic Irish behaviour. We were wrong. The coach driver snapped. He stopped the coach, opened the door and leapt down the stairs, then launched an apoplectic stream of obscenity at the object of his seemingly boundless rage.

It was stupendous. The compiler of a thesaurus could have greatly expanded the entries under profanity, personal injury, reproduction, human genitalia and all forms of bodily excretion. The tirade went on and on. When the driver finally climbed back aboard the coach, his face was violet and spittle flecked his chin. There was an appalled silence. I suspect quite a few of the Americans would have liked to abandon the tour and walk back to town. First, though, they'd have to get past the coach driver. No one moved.

The driver said nothing. He engaged the gears, closed the doors and manoeuvred past the van. Then he resumed his chatty commentary with absolutely no reference to what had just happened.

The tour took about eight hours, during which we took one photo. This was not the fault of the scenery. There were plenty of great views, lookouts and places of interest around this renowned coastal drive. But the coach drove past them all. It may have been because our schedule had been upset, or because it meant we could spend more time at all the coach-stop cafés, eateries and souvenir shops along the way, none of which coincided with a scenic viewpoint. Short of taking snaps from the moving bus, we were reduced to considering taking pictures of cheap trinkets or the cowed expressions of our fellow passengers. Some of them obviously hadn't gotten over the morning. When the driver said 'Please be back in the coach in ten minutes', everyone was back in their seats in five.

The subdued mood was also in part due to the Ring itself. There was an air of desolation about the place, which grew heavier as the day went on. At one valley the driver explained that the surrounding area had once had a population estimated at 100,000, but today it was only a few hundred as the result of starvation and mass emigration after the potato famine of the nineteenth century. This was mirrored throughout Ireland: before the famine, its population was estimated at nine million. After the famine it fell to three million and to this day it has only recovered to about four million. In fact, the population only began to grow in the 1990s as Ireland's booming economy, the Celtic Tiger, lured people back. Much of the prosperity centres on Dublin, but in the west coast the sense of being at the scene of a tragedy persists. The country around the Ring of Kerry was as green as the rest of Ireland, but it was scarred by jagged rocks in every field. It was like looking at the bones of a starving man.

Of course, one person's desolation is another's nirvana, especially for those with religious or spiritual leanings. And as it happens, just off the Kerry coast there's a place that's not only desolate, it's got spiritual leanings with bells on.

Skellig Michael (Archangel Michael's Rock) and Little Skellig (presumably Little Rock, no relation to Arkansas) are two guano-encrusted fangs of stone which protrude from the sea about ten kilometres from the tip of the Ring. Rising sheer from the water, they look like the inspiration for a fantasy illustrator's images of the desolate haunts of dragons, sorcerers and imprisoned maidens awaiting rescue. These unpromising bits of real estate became the home of Christian monks from the sixth century onwards. A lot of early Christians liked their religion good and hard, and the monks reckoned that denial and isolation helped them devote their thoughts and actions to God. They sure hit the jackpot with the Skelligs, where the monastery and stone beehive huts are perched halfway up a 270-metre rock in the middle of the ocean.

The monks also had a lot to do with saving Christianity's bacon. Around the sixth century, the Roman Empire had gone pretty well pear-shaped and as a result couldn't stop various pagan hordes who were hell-bent on sweeping Christendom off the map. But in Ireland, the hard men of monasteries like the one on the Skelligs (and they were all blokes) weren't so easy to budge. For starters you needed a pretty good boat just to get at them. Not only that, but sitting on a bare rock with just God, birds and other monks for company, they ended up getting quite a bit of reading done. In fact, they ended up being the best-read people in Europe, particularly since they got sent lots of precious texts for safe-keeping. So whenever the heat died down the monks would travel back into Europe, spreading the word and educating people about things like reading, writing and not killing everyone they met. It was because of them that Ireland became known as a land of poets and scholars.

I find these guys pretty impressive for a couple of reasons. First, I can identify with people who spent their days in a drafty cell, hunched over a manuscript. Second, they kept the light of civilisation burning for centuries while everyone else was a-rapin' and a-pillagin'. These days, when someone's always saying 'We'll all be ruined', it's comforting to know that it only takes a handful of people to sustain the idea of a better world.

The monks stayed on the Skelligs for six or seven hundred years and they're known to have withstood at least two Viking raids in the ninth century, which saw some of them killed or taken as slaves. No one knows why they eventually abandoned the settlement. Maybe after 600 years they were sick to death of a diet of fish. The stone huts and buildings are still there, empty and windswept, but the rock is now only a home for seabirds. Mind you, if I had the opportunity to stay there for six months I'd grab it like a shot. I'd go in the winter and write a book I've had in mind for some time. Where's it set? The Australian desert. Well, if Joyce went to Europe to write about Dublin, it seems reasonable to go to Skellig Michael to write about the great southern land.

To my disappointment, the bus didn't stop at a place where we could get a good picture of the Skelligs. The only place it stopped where there was a good picture was at the end of the day, at the Lady's View. This was where Queen Victoria took in the view of the lakes. It was fairly scenic, although the heavy clouds rolling in made the outlook more gloomy than spectacular. Still, it was a chance for a snap, so we took it.

BACK AT THE hostel we found that, despite the schism that now existed between us, anticlockwise travellers did have their uses. They had information about what was ahead. In the generally convivial atmosphere of hostels, people travelling in the opposite direction are a great resource on all of the places you are about to visit – good and bad places, good and bad experiences. That night we met some anticlockwise people who had also been to the Ring of Kerry but said the Dingle Peninsula (just to the north) was just as scenic. It was also easier to manage because it was much smaller. You could ride right around it on a pushbike in a day. Not only that, but just outside of town there was a good hostel with a great view over the sea. It sounded good. But could the anticlockwisers be trusted?

I was torn. I wanted to take a boat to the Skelligs, so I could imagine spending six months there. And maybe if we spent more time in Killarney we might actually manage to try more than one pub. But Dingle beckoned.

Then the anticlockwisers told us something that clinched it. 'Dingle is quite a small town,' they said. 'It has a population of only 1,270 but it's got 52 pubs.'

We decided to make a move.

6

PUB TOWN

It didn't take us long to discover that the road to Dingle was definitely one less travelled. We'd been told that getting there was a toss-up between hitchhiking and public transport – there was a bus service that was fairly unreliable, but the same could be said of hitchhiking. And there were so many hitchhikers the locals were sick of picking them up. We decided to take the cheaper option, which ended up costing us dearly.

From Killarney we hitched to the town of Castlemaine pretty easily. Then a local took us as far as his farm gate, dropping us on a long straight stretch of road in the middle of nowhere. It wasn't a good place for hitchhiking, but you couldn't argue with the setting. Dingle Bay was behind us, farmhouses clung to the green and gentle slopes of the evocatively if incomprehensibly named Slieve Mish Mountains. We propped our bags against an ancient-looking stone wall and waited for a car to pick us up.

Two hours later we were still there. By then we'd experienced the full range of Irish weather – dry, then damp, then wet, followed by soaking wet, torrential, and biblical downpour complete with detailed schematic of Ark. We'd watched the colours and light change on the aforementioned Slieve Mish Mountains, then we'd watched them change back again. We'd played frisbee. Twidkiwodm discovered that it was actually possible for me to run out of jokes and become despondent. I'd even made up a few new ones, such as 'Why did the hitchhiker cross the road?' Yes, we'd become very bored.

You may recall that I mentioned in Chapter 2 that if an appropriate moment came up I'd explain how I manage to travel with minimal luggage for weeks on end. Well, that time has come. And no skipping ahead:

imagine you're stuck with us on the roadside and can't get away.

OK. At the very bottom of the daypack, which zips down both sides so I can get at anything I need without pulling everything out, is my sheet sleeping bag. A sheet sleeping bag is just that – a sheet sewn into a bag, which you use in hostels so they don't have to (or in case they never do) change the sheets.

Next, a pair of jeans, a pair of shorts, a pair of socks and a T-shirt. In other words, one full change of clothes with the shorts for warm weather and/or athletic activities.

Underwear is an issue unto itself. I run a one-underpants, one-pair-of-togs strategy. Swimmers dry quickly, so I wear them most of the time and rinse them out as necessary. If I get caught in the rare situation where they're wet, the underpants come into play. There are, of course, other underpants strategies. For example, there's the four-days'-wear-from-one-pair strategy – underpants forward, then underpants backward, then inside-out forward, then inside-out backward. I prefer my strategy. It's a lot less crusty and you always have fresh, dry smalls.

On top of the clothes I have a small towel, a lightweight jumper, and usually on top of that my waterproof jacket, folded up tight and at the top front of the pack. At the back is my toiletries bag (toothbrush, toothpaste, shampoo, razor, razor blades, shaving cream, comb). The jacket and toiletries bag, being waterproof, tend to keep everything below them dry in the event of a sudden downburst. Assuming, that is, that most rain falls downwards. If the rain's blowing sideways, hopefully I'm running for shelter. This assumes, too, that if it's started raining, it's also cold and the jumper is being worn, and so being kept dry by me having run for shelter. And if it's warm rain it means I'm not in Ireland but in the tropics and don't need the jumper anyway.

That's the essentials taken care of. I am, of course, wearing my second set of clothes and my only pair of shoes. My little extras include a frisbee. This, as I've already demonstrated, is a compact toy for exercise and entertainment (especially when girls like Katrin and Twidkiwodm are involved). At a pinch it can also double as a plate when having an impromptu roadside picnic, say when waiting for someone, anyone, anything to stop and give us a ride.

I also carry juggling balls, for two reasons. First, I can juggle. Second, people may be more likely to stop for jugglers. They think, 'Hey, a juggler. Not a deranged psychopath. I'll stop.'

In the front pocket of the daypack I have a few handy items. A Swiss army knife with corkscrew, bottle and can opener. Maps of the country or area being travelled in. Two pens. A couple of small notebooks. (As I fill these up I mail them home to my family, so they can follow my adventures and the notes will be there ready for the day a publisher says 'Hey, wanna write a travel book?'.)

Sometimes I also have one of those 'traveller novels'. These are books that get left behind at hostels when people finish them and are then picked up by someone else who leaves it at another hostel, etc., etc. Often people write in their names and the places they took the book to, so you get a little diary of its travels. Some of them have been all over the world.

There are two other books tucked into the pack. One is a travel guide to the country I'm in. The other is a book called *Sydney's Poems*, which tucks neatly into the frisbee, which slides down the inside back of the pack. It's there in case I feel homesick. It contains a favourite, 'Five Bells' by Kenneth Slessor, about a friend of his who drowned in Sydney Harbour. I just have to read it and I'm home, sailing around the buoys on a summer afternoon or picnicking on a warm evening at Mrs Macquarie's Chair, with the harbour and the Opera House spread before me. Another poem I quite like is on the back of the book. It's a small one by W.H. Auden, which isn't about Sydney but is about poetry. This is all of it:

A poet's hope:
to be like some valley cheese,
local but prized elsewhere.

Reading poetry, or memorising slabs of it, is another good way to kill time until someone stops to give you a ride, which on this occasion they eventually did after three hours.

The people who picked us up were from Northern Ireland. They were tourists, a couple in their thirties, and they never picked up hitchhikers.

'It's the first toim John has ever stopped. It moost be yer looky day.' After five hours, during which we'd only travelled forty kilometres, it didn't feel like it.

The drive to Dingle took less than half an hour and was, as we'd been told, as scenic as anything on the Ring of Kerry. We drove through Inch, with its long sandy strand and sweeping lines of breakers. Then we climbed into the mountains, cut inland through a small pass and were greeted by the sight of a rich and fertile valley with a patchwork of green fields. It looked like paradise.

Not far down the road we got dropped off at the road that led to the Seacrest Hostel. When we eventually arrived, we discovered a converted nineteenth-century farmhouse set high on a hill overlooking the sweep of Dingle Bay and the Blasket Islands beyond. The anticlockwisers hadn't let us down – we liked it immediately. Even better, the distance from town seemed to filter out the people who put practical considerations before aesthetics, the result being a group of guests who all seemed interesting in their own ways.

The hostel's immediate environs had a few points of interest of their own. After organising our beds for the night, we went exploring on the hillside above the hostel. The manager, a chatty New Zealander named Tom, told us there were megalithic tombs up there, dating back some 3,000 years. He pointed them out on a survey map which also made it pretty clear that we were in the middle of an area littered with ancient sites – ring forts, tombs and standing stones.

Dingle has more of them than nearly anywhere else in Ireland.

We eventually found the tombs we thought we were looking for although considering how many sites there were, we couldn't be sure. They were formed by several large flat slabs of rock, roughly hewn, and those of us with no idea how long it takes a body to decompose expected to find some evidence of human bodies inside. But there was only grass and bracken: apparently 3,000 years is more than long enough.

We poked around for a while, then just settled down amid the tombs and tussocks to enjoy the view. The afternoon sun was warm and the hillside was covered in wildflowers. To the west, headland after jagged headland stretched out along the peninsula. In the distance to the south, the long finger of coast and peaks of the Ring of Kerry stretched to a low mountain that finally sloped to the water, marking the very edge of Europe. We had it all to ourselves – just us and the dead.

BACK AT THE hostel, the distance from Dingle had somehow failed to deter a less aesthetically inclined visitor, who was rapidly establishing himself as a nuisance. He was loud, obnoxious and, to our great shame, Australian. A lot of people stereotype Australian men as pigs, which is generally regarded as a bit unfair. In this case it was unfair to pigs.

Nuisance particularly found the mixed dormitory rooms a great novelty. 'This is my bed, girls,' he said at the top of his voice, to no one in particular, 'so you know where I'll be tonight.' When he wasn't looking, a couple of young women moved their gear to another room. Instinctively, we kept our voices down so that he couldn't hear us speak. The last thing we wanted was for him to catch our accents and start treating us as friends and countrymen.

In the evening, the hostel ran a shuttle into town so people could go to the pubs and restaurants. It was no surprise that Nuisance was one of the passengers in the minibus, jabbering away to anyone and everyone, all of whom sat in enduring silence.

As soon as the bus hit town, the passengers dispersed rapidly in a 'the other way from you' manner. We also gave Nuisance the slip and strolled around the town counting the pubs, trying to decide which one to try first. Dick Mack's, opposite the church, was perhaps the town's best known. It spruiks itself colourfully on the outside, but inside it's still the original pub – old and wooden, with a bar on one side and a shoe repairer on the other. It was still early in the evening, but a couple of musicians were playing to a handful of customers. We bought a couple of half-pints and found a little spot on the shoe side of the bar. No one minded us much although the room was so small you couldn't help but eavesdrop on every conversation.

'Gee, I wonder what this place is like when it's crowded?' I said.

Twidkiwodm glanced at me. 'You're not going to start doing jokes about shoe-horning customers in, are you?'

'I wasn't going to,' I protested. 'What sort of heel do you take me for?'

Dick Mack's pulled a good Guinness. It was so good we were tempted to stay and have a proper pint but rather than settle in at the first pub we came to we thought we should at least look around a bit more. Eventually, we drifted down the hill towards the docks where dozens of fishing boats were tied up. On the road opposite the docks we weren't surprised to find more pubs. The town is nearly one long bar. We went into one we liked the look of: Maeve de Barra's.

At first, we didn't notice all the people who'd come

from the hostel, because they were quite hard to see. They were at a table that was all but hidden in a 'snug' behind the front door.

'He isn't with you?' one of them asked when we stopped to say hello.

'No. And we made sure he isn't following us.'

They invited us to join them.

We ordered a couple of pints and settled down at the table while the barman poured. There were half a dozen people, including a couple of German girls, Miriam and Marianne, and two Italian boys, Marco and Michele.

'We'd have asked you to come with us earlier, but we thought you were with him.'

'Whatever gave you that idea?'

'You're all Australians.'

'And that,' Twidkiwodm explained, 'is where the connection ends.'

When they were ready, I went and got the pints. Back at the table, with the first taste the flavour of creamy roasted barley bit my tongue and seized my attention. 'Ah,' I sighed, settling back in my seat. After a long day, my body was starting to say, 'Come on, it's beer o'clock. Let's just sit here for a bit and stop running around.'

Fine by me. I let the conversation flow around me, watching strangers from Germany, Italy, Australia and even Ireland gradually become friends. The only distraction was the front door, which diverted everyone's attention whenever someone came in. As soon as we knew it wasn't Nuisance, the conversation resumed.

It turned out that Miriam and Marianne had hired bikes from the hostel and ridden over the Connor Pass, one of the highest in Ireland. It had almost killed them. However, the road around the peninsula avoided the mountains and took in all the major sights, which made it a better bet. At their suggestion, Twidkiwodm and I decided to ride the peninsula the next morning.

Then the conversation turned to Guinness. Miriam started telling me about a pub in Galway that was famous for its Guinness because it was still served in stone jugs. They were a hangover, so to speak, from the old days. When I asked the name of the pub, she couldn't remember but she assured me the place was well known. Everything was falling neatly into place. Stone-jug pub, somewhere in Galway. We'd go and find it as soon as we got there. Meanwhile, we still had the pubs of Dingle awaiting us – O'Flaherty's,

Murphy's, the An Conair, the An Droisead Beag and Doyle's, to name just a tenth of them.

Around closing time we headed off to catch the last minibus back to the hostel. We all piled in and the driver did a head-count. He came up one short. Nuisance.

'Do you want us to go and look for him?'

'No, we'll give 'im foiv minutes.'

We gave him five minutes, then five more.

'Leave him,' someone piped up. 'Let him walk.'

'Oim sorrly tempted,' the driver said.

After we'd sat in the dark for twenty minutes, we saw a figure staggering towards us, gripped in what appeared to be its own personal windstorm. When he got to the bus, Nuisance dragged open the door and half-fell into the vehicle. 'Geez I'm pissed,' he explained as he slumped into a seat.

No one said anything. The driver started the engine but unfortunately, the vibration of the vehicle must have set off a chain reaction. Nuisance farted: long and loud. 'Better out than in,' he said. Everyone agreed with him and despite the chilly night we slid the windows open. Soon the air was as cold as the silence. But it stank a lot less.

THE NEXT MORNING, the management of the hostel told Nuisance there was no room at the inn and they didn't have a manger. As he was leaving we noted that he was travelling anticlockwise. We tried not to let this reinforce our prejudices (about anticlockwise people, that is), but we knew it meant he was gone from our lives forever.

In the meantime, we seized the day. Or more precisely, we seized the handlebars of a couple of bicycles. I soon discovered that riding with stitches in my hand was a tricky business. It was only comfortable if I kept my hand flat on the handlebar, rather than gripping it, but that meant I could only keep balance on that side and lightly steer. I couldn't use the brakes very well either, which made for a couple of corners where I barely avoided adding to my stock of souvenir scar-tissue.

It was a lot easier on the flat as we pushed through Dingle and on towards Slea Head. We rolled along with green fields on one side, the Atlantic on the other (going clockwise). As we rode we were on the lookout both for beehive huts and for the tourist cars that were paying more attention to the view than to the road.

Apparently, Dingle's beehive huts leave the Skellig

beehives for dead, particularly when it comes to their age. They're reputed to be 3,000–4,000 years old, which has to be some kind of record for huts. The first lot were in a farmer's field. At the front gate the farmer's wife was asking a pound for a closer look, though you could see the huts clearly from the road. She was doing quite good business, but she didn't seem very happy about it. I suspect it was because people forked over their money for the huts and then abused her for not delivering more; or perhaps they didn't pay and accused her of being a profiteer. We really wanted to see the beehive huts, so we paid up and shut up. Even then she didn't seem at all grateful.

The huts were constructed using hundreds of stones stacked, without mortar, in a cunning arrangement that closed in at the top and formed a roof. They looked like they should collapse or let the rain in, but they turned out to be pretty dry. And they'd been that way for thousands of years, which is why there are a couple of Sydney builders I'd like to show them to. It was only when we pedalled a little further on and found more huts, unattended, that we realised we could look at huts for free. We didn't particularly mind. It was a fairly modest donation to make to the local economy and more than compensated by the dramatic scenery that unfolded near Slea Head. Out to sea the Blasket Islands loomed out of a slight mist. They were rugged, though not as stark as the Skelligs except for the jagged tooth known as Tearaght.

The Blaskets have inspired quite a few books, some of which were responsible for the resurgence of pride in Irish heritage at the start of the twentieth century. Among the writers was Peig Sayers, an island woman and story-teller whose autobiography, *Peig*, dictated to her son, tells how hard they used to do it out there. It's pretty compelling stuff. In fact, it's so compelling that people stopped living on the Blaskets in 1953.

The road clung to sheer cliffs as it rounded the southern tip of the peninsula. Then, ranging into the distance, were four mountains that looked like they'd been sliced in half. They sloped up to their peaks then dropped sheer for hundreds of metres into the swirling ocean below. There weren't many fences on the edges of the cliffs. Perhaps they weren't needed because the local sheep were smart enough to stay away from the edge. Or else the cliffs were tumbling into the sea so frequently they were taking the fences with them, along with the odd quadruped. The fields were still dotted with the luckier sheep and with stone cottages that had great views over the wild waters of the Atlantic. Several looked ideal as places to retreat to if you were a writer who'd grabbed the chance to live on the Skelligs only to find it was one of the stupidest ideas you'd ever had.

At the tiny seaside village of Dunquin we had a rest. We found a café with views across to the Blaskets. Inside they served big pots of tea and digestive biscuits. While we looked, slurped and munched we got talking to the proprietor, mainly about whether the paintings of the islands she was trying to hang were straight and why she needed them when she could see the same thing out of her window. 'For the tourists,' she said.

'Or if there's fog,' I suggested.

While we were talking, a car pulled up and two American couples got out. 'Is it open?' an acutely nasal women started to bray, though she was standing beside a sign that said 'OPEN'. Then she and her friends bugled their way into the café. 'What's inside?' 'The Blaskets! What are they?!' 'Roger, look over here!'

If it came to fog, they could have used this woman to warn shipping.

From Dunquin we pedalled on to one of the peninsula's significant historic sites, the Riasc monastic settlement. It was in a field, accessed free of charge by climbing a stone wall. As there was no attendant present I've no idea how to pronounce Riasc. At a guess it might be 'Re-ask' or 'Rash' or 'Rack'. Knowing Irish pronunciation it could just as easily be 'Keep guessing'.

The place certainly left us guessing about what it must have once been like. In its time, the signs said, Riasc was one of the oldest and most substantial monastic settlements in the area. These days, though, it consists of low walls of small rocks that seem to separate what excites archaeologists from what excites your average punter. At least with things like the beehive huts you had actual structures to help you imagine how the settlements might have looked. At Riasc all you had to build an image with were the foundations.

Down the road from Riasc we found a pub where we had lunch and what I calculated would be the most westerly pints of Guinness we could manage. In our quest for the perfect pint, this was a significant moment. If those Dubliners who'd said the best Guinness was in the west were right, the proof may well be nigh. For starters Tig Bric (Brick's Pub) did a very nice toasted ham and cheese sandwich. Not too hot, generous with the cheese. Pepper on the side if you wanted it. The Guinness went down very easily – smooth on the mid-palate, smoky on the back palate – a most satisfying pint. But was it perfect? Well, we had no cause for complaint, and yet – as in Maeve de Barra's, Dick Mack's, An Conair or The Laurels in Killarney – it didn't taste radically different from the Dublin variety. We had just the one pint, what with being on the bikes and sufficiently injured already not to want to add to the casualty count. Plus we wanted to give ourselves plenty of time for the peninsula's most important sight, which was just ahead of us.

Imagining monks keeping the light of civilisation burning was easy at the Gallarus Oratory, one of the world's most ingenious buildings. It was built in about the seventh century, using stone blocks fitted together like an intricate jigsaw puzzle. And again no mortar was used: the building is supported mostly by the pure skill of its artisans, the four sides closing in to join at a ridge about four metres high. The blocks are also carefully placed so that they slope slightly outwards, keeping it dry inside when it rains. The same techniques were used for the beehive huts, which predate it by a couple of thousand years, but the superior construction of the Oratory makes them look like… well, huts really.

The Oratory was on its own in a little field a short walk from the video theatre, gift shop and sundry tourism accoutrements. And keeping it company, leaning against the stone wall that enclosed the field, was an old man and a collie dog. The man had no teeth. I can't speak for the dog.

When Twidkiwodm started to take the man's photo, he started shouting and waving. We couldn't understand a word he said. We knew we were in a Gaeltacht, so he may have been speaking Gaelic. On the other hand, it may just have been gummy English.

'Do you mind if I take your photo?' Twidkiwodm asked him.

'Shluffle begoshnek ashen shlubbledribble.'

She turned to me. 'Was that a yes or a no?'

'Just hurry up and take it, if that's what you want to do.'

She clicked. He babbled. We left.

FOR ME, THE other highlight of the Dingle Peninsula was looming behind the Oratory. Mt Brandon, at 951 metres Ireland's second-highest peak, gets its name from a variation on the name of Brendan, yet another monk (a saint, too), who is thought to have sailed a leather boat to America with 17 other monks some time in the sixth century. He is supposed to have set off from Brandon Creek at the foot of the mountain, one of the most westerly launching points in Europe.

Brendan's exploits are detailed in a book called *Navigatio Sancti Brendani Abbatis* (The Voyage of Saint Brendan the Abbot), which exists in various manuscripts dating from around the eighth century. However, his accounts of his adventures – encounters with floating pillars of crystal and fire-breathing monsters, for example – have led many scholars to opine 'Pull the other one, it plays jingle bells', albeit in more scholarly terms. The fanciful descriptions do make it sound like Brendan may have been on a trip, though not necessarily one to America. So, the academic and adventurer Tim Severin built a replica of Brendan's boat, based on the traditional Irish currach, and attempted the voyage in 1976. He reached Newfoundland in 1977, illuminating many of the obscure descriptions in the Navigatio – the pillars of crystal might be icebergs, the fire-breathing monsters spouting whales. He concluded that

Brendan really could have done it. Severin was a great admirer of the early Irish monks, whom he also saw as the repository not only of Christianity but of all knowledge. His book, *The Brendan Voyage*, is a wonderful adventure. The boat he travelled in is still around, too, at the Craggaunowen Project in County Clare.

Whoever named Ireland's mountains must have thought pretty highly of Brendan too. We got first-hand experience of how high as the road climbed one of Brandon's massive flanks, our own flanks burning with the effort, to a pass that sat on the spine of the peninsula. When we crested the rise we stopped to catch our breath and check out the view.

'Thank God. It's all downhill from here,' Twidkiwodm gasped.

Ahead of us the road ribboned across the farmland towards Dingle. Even better, the wind was at our backs. I estimated we'd pedalled about forty kilometres, which was pretty good considering our preparation for this sort of activity had mainly involved the flexing of arm and throat muscles.

We got going again but not long after I noticed Twidkiwodm starting to look for any excuse to stop.

She was starting to flag and if I wasn't careful, she'd flag down a lift back to town and leave me with the hikes. Fortunately, the road lacked significant distractions until we came upon a patch of blackberries and Twidkiwodm insisted we pick some. Behind us some wet-looking clouds were closing in, so I started getting pushy. I cursed my failure to carry a whip with which to help my companion along the path to adventure as my admonitions flowed like water off a tired cyclist's back.

'You have to decide,' I insisted. 'Berries or staying dry.'

Twidkiwodm chose berries. As we picked them, a car passed and I caught a glimpse of two kids looking at us out of the back window of the car. Their faces were a mixture of suspicion and envy. I wondered if they thought I was the evil berry-picker.

We got back to Dingle dry anyway and went for a coffee at An Cafe Liteartha (which I'm prepared to bet is Gaelic for The Literary Café), where I bought an English translation of Peig Sayers' book. And later that night I was literally made to eat my words over the berries – mixed with some sugar and yoghurt, they made a fine dessert.

NOT ALL BACKPACKERS are untidy, but it's a universal law of communal kitchens that if you didn't dirty it you don't have to wash it up. Which means that it only takes a few dirty things to start a snowball effect that can send a clean kitchen down the slippery slope to a congealed mass of dishes, pots and pans.

At breakfast the next morning, Seacrest's kitchen was that unsavoury snowball. After all our bike riding, Twidkiwodm and I had decided to have a lazy day washing our clothes, and since she was having a long hot shower and I was just sitting around, I decided, 'Stuff it, I'll clean this place.'

So I started washing dishes. A couple of people were hanging around as well, but I soon recruited them for the drying up with vivid descriptions of a pristine kitchen nirvana. You might like to think about that for a moment. Meanwhile, we were getting the place pretty spick. And span wasn't far off.

As we washed and chatted, a couple of English girls came in and started making breakfast. Eventually one of them said, 'Excuse me. Are you really Australian?'

'Yeah,' I replied. 'Why?'

'You're washing up,' she said. 'I thought all Australian men were lazy pigs.'

I told you it was a stereotype. I lifted a trotter from the sink, scratched my snout and grunted. Obviously the margin between lazy pig and dish pig was rasher-thin. But then I suppose every country has its clichéd character. I freely admit that I used to think all English men were soccer hooligans. But it wasn't until I went to England that I discovered that some English men don't like soccer.

THE KITCHEN WAS gleaming and I was still waiting for Twidkiwodm when I got talking to a man from England who was holidaying with his two children. The thing you couldn't help noticing about Paul was that he had a hook where most of us have a left hand. The hook had the ability to open and close, like pincers, and gleamed as only surgical appliances can. It looked quite new, but the rest of Paul was in his thirties and was topped with red-blond hair and a face that looked like it had spent a lot of time outdoors.

We got along from the moment we started talking, not least because we both had stories to tell about hand injuries. When Paul found out we weren't planning to do much that day, he invited us to come with him and his kids on a drive through

the Connor Pass to Castlegregory. It sounded good
to me and when Twidkiwodm appeared she agreed.
So much for a quiet day at the hostel. If this kept
up, I was going to have to rethink my underpants
strategy. Paul went to round up his kids. Heri was
a 14-year-old boy/man with the tense air of
someone coming to grips with making the
transition between the two. In other words, a lot
of the time he seemed to want to be somewhere
other than on holiday with his dad and sister Kobi.
She was a year younger and a lot more comfortable
about who she was. Having been in the company
of her father and brother for a couple of weeks,
though, she took to Twidkiwodm like a duck to
water – a big sister for the day. The whispering
started before we'd left the hostel car park.

Paul's vehicle turned out to be a large campervan
– although recreational omnibus would be a more
accurate description. It was laden with camping
equipment, a windsurfer, a small inflatable dinghy
with outboard motor and sundry paraphernalia.

I was particularly interested to see how Paul
managed the vehicle with only one hand and a hook.
However, the vehicle's only modification was a knob
on the steering wheel, which Paul could hook onto

and use to pull the wheel around. Driving was a piece of cake.

This was just as well, because pretty soon we were climbing the even steeper winding road to the Connor Pass. Actually, 'road' is a bit of an overstatement – even 'narrow track' is flattering – and as it got higher, it got narrower and the drop beside us got bigger. How big was the drop? So big I've got a nosebleed just writing about it. The pass itself was wedged between cliffs and rocky treeless mountains. A grey mist clung to the peaks and the road was wet with rain. It beats me how the road got wet as the wind was blowing so hard the rain wasn't falling, it was going sideways. There was a lookout, but no takers in the cold and rain. Or maybe there had been but the elements had plucked them away. Back at the hostel the sun had been shining. Up here it was a different world.

On the other side of the pass, the road was hacked out of the cliff. This was a stretch Tom at the hostel had told us about. Sometimes it was so dark and misty that he reckoned locals navigated by driving with an arm out the window, feeling for the rock. On the opposite side of the road there was nothing. If you leaned right over you could just make out a stream swirling over jagged rocks far below. Or so I was told.

We crept along, both so we could take in the sights and because we were scared we were going to miss a corner and plunge into a ravine. Eventually the valley started to widen and then to the north the view opened out across a vast sweep of green hills rolling to a line of distant blue sea.

One of the reasons Paul wanted to check out the town of Castlegregory was that the area was famous for its windsurfing regattas. I was interested because it was the town where John Moriarty, an Aborigine I'd worked with on the book *Saltwater Fella*, had found his Irish relatives. He'd actually sat down there with someone he susupected was his cousin and started looking at old photos. Then he saw a picture of something he recognised – his mother, standing on the balcony of the pub at Borroloola in the Northern Territory. His cousin pointed to another figure and said 'That's my uncle.' It was John's father (who had since died), whom he'd never known and had taken 40 years to trace.

We looked around the town for a while and then went exploring in a graveyard, because if it's history you're after they're usually crawling with it (among other things). Unlike Dingle's megalithic tombs, some of the graves in Castlegregory still had old bones in them. Usually the dead are kept well out of sight but this place seemed to have a more casual attitude. Or maybe it's an Irish thing: everywhere you go in Ireland the dead make their presence felt; the landscape is chock-full of tombs, graves and monuments. Perhaps this exposure puts the living more at ease with those who aren't. Or perhaps there are so many generations, tombs, historic sites and relics that if the living tried to keep it all buried they wouldn't have time for anything else.

Not far from the cemetery we found a small lake that looked like it was perfectly suited to more active pursuits, such as windsurfing. Paul was itching to go. I was scratching for an excuse to avoid it. What was it the doctor in Killarney said about trouble? I'd gone rowing and cycling, both without doing any serious damage, but windsurfing? That might be going a little too far. Then I thought about Paul. If he could do it with one hand and a hook, who was I to cavil about a couple of stitches and a mere scratch?

'Oh what the hell. Bring it on,' I replied. We started unloading the gear.

This was yet another of those situations where using your swimming togs as underwear comes in handy. You never know when you might want to go swimming and if you're already wearing your togs, you're all set up. That is, unless it's cold as charity and you're rigging up a sailboard clad only in swimmers and T-shirt. Paul wrestled on the only wetsuit while I practised shivering so that later, when I fell in, I'd be ready.

How does a man with a hook handle a windsurfer? Like he handles a van. Paul had a harness that supported most of his weight, so all he had to do with his hand and hook was fine-tune his balance. When he took off, though, I couldn't help wondering whether there was anything this guy couldn't do. I finally concluded it was likely he'd be stymied by Rachmaninoff's *Third Piano Concerto*. Of course, the fact I couldn't play a note of it was neither here nor there.

All too soon it was my turn. In view of its injury, we wrapped my hand in a plastic bag and put an elastic band around it, to keep it dry. The result looked as ludicrous as it was inadequate. So between my hand and the freezing conditions, I decided the best strategy was to concentrate on trying to avoid falling into the water. Considering the strength of the wind and the fact that Paul had a full-sized rather than a storm sail, it was going to take some doing.

After pulling on the wetsuit I grabbed the board and waded into deeper water. Then it really hit me. The lake was arctic. I shrank even further from the idea of falling in, some bits of me more than others. But, miraculously, my plan succeeded. You can keep your rats leaving sinking ships. Sure there were a few ungraceful moments, but they were a small price to pay for staying dry. Eventually I worked my way upwind a bit and let rip with some high-speed reaching runs. The board bounded across the wave tops like a skipping stone.

'Pretty good. You didn't fall in once,' Paul said when I got back to the jetty.

I shrugged and tried to appear nonchalant, which isn't easy when you're convulsed with shivers. Twidkiwodm didn't help much. 'Normally he does tricks,' she said. 'Why aren't you showing off, you puss?' Well it was easy for her: she was standing on the dock wearing a couple of woolly jumpers.

We swapped the wetsuit. As we watched Paul's second run, the sun broke from behind a curtain of rain that was drifting towards us from the Connor Pass. It turned the surface of the lake to mercury. Then Paul tucked into a big gust and got the board flying. Even from a distance we could hear it thumping across the tops of the waves. There was spray all round him and a huge wake spread behind. It looked like something Turner would have painted, except for the windsurfer.

WHEN IT'S JUST two of you travelling around, breakfast is usually a fairly straightforward affair – a cup of tea, a bowl of cereal and thou. But breakfast at Seacrest was becoming a major production – Paul and his kids, Marco, Michele, Miriam, Marianne and us.

It wasn't going to last, though, as the Italians were leaving to go sightseeing around Tralee. They were keen for us to go too, but Paul and the kids had already asked us to spend another day with them. 'Maybe we'll catch you up,' we said, knowing there was a good chance of it since we were all travelling clockwise.

Meanwhile, aquatic pursuits continued to dominate the agenda. Since 1983 a bottlenose dolphin named Fungie has been hanging around the mouth of Dingle harbour, and since Paul had a dinghy among his impressive recreational arsenal, after breakfast we drove down to the harbour and set up the boat and its little outboard. Paul took the kids out first and they returned exhilarated. So naturally I offered Twidkiwodm the chance to go next. She declined. In fact she insisted I go first. It turned out to be a smart move.

Moments after Paul and I embarked, we discovered the reason why. The vessel, being tiny, succumbed to our combined weight and folded in half. Paul and I slid together into a tangled pile, shipping water from both sides. After a concerted effort to push ourselves apart, followed by a rubbery 'sproing', the dinghy regained a resemblance to what's usually referred to in the maritime business as 'shipshape'. Trying to arrange ourselves a little more comfortably only led to more mayhem. Then I let out an almighty yelp of pain: something was biting me. It felt like a crab had my little toe in its claws and as I leapt to escape its pincers, the boat folded in half again. Then I looked down and saw that the pincers belonged to Paul's hook. The spring was so strong it was like being caught in a vice.

'You've got my toe!' I shouted, as the boat filled with water and we struggled to get apart.

'Sorry!' Paul frantically opened the pincers to release me. 'I couldn't feel it.'

While we bailed out the water, we couldn't help

laughing. Not surprisingly, the commotion we were causing attracted the attention of Fungie. He suddenly appeared beside us, having deserted a boat full of fish-tossing tourists, and as he slid through the water alongside the little dinghy he seemed huge, at least twice its length.

Paul told me to poke an oar into the water as we putted along and Fungie swam beside us, just beneath the surface. He moved up close to the oar and let it scratch his skin. Then he slid under the dinghy and swam beneath us, making the boat flex and surf on the pressure wave above his back. That is, until we nosed into the water, shipped a large piece of the Atlantic and folded in half again. More struggling and splashing.

When we got going again, Fungie slid back under us. Though we feared the outboard would turn his dorsal fin to sashimi, he somehow managed to keep it out of harm's way as he played with us like a waterlogged cork.

For Twidkiwodm's turn, Paul let the two of us go back out together. I was at the back of the dinghy, on what could laughably be called the helm, when Fungie came zipping back across the bay. When he arrived, to say he was interested in Twidkiwodm was an understatement. For a while he cruised along beside us, looking up at her from just below the surface. Then, it seemed this wasn't enough. He stopped swimming and stuck his upper body out of the water beside her so he could have a good long look. I'd always thought Twidkiwodm had a fair bit of 'presence' about her. Fungie seemed to think so, too. I actually felt a pang of jealousy. And there aren't many people who've been jealous of an aquatic mammal.

But Fungie still had one more trick up his fin. When he got bored playing with us, he slid down into the depths and disappeared. We slapped the water with the oars for a while, hoping to lure him back, but there wasn't a sign. So we turned around and started to head back to shore. Then suddenly Fungie leapt out of the water right beside us. We yelped in surprise as he soared in front of the dinghy and then hit the water with the dolphin equivalent of a belly-flop, dispensing yet another soaking. Then he shot through, with what sounded suspiciously like a soggy snigger.

LATER, HEADING UP the road from the water we noticed that a crowd was gathering at what we hadn't noticed was a racetrack when we'd driven by earlier in the morning. It had just looked like another field on the slope overlooking the harbour. It was a Saturday afternoon and most of the town and district seemed to be assembling. The field was gradually filling with cars, fish-and-chip vans, bookies and the odd horse. We decided such spontaneity shouldn't go unnoticed and stopped to have a look.

Despite Ireland's enormous reputation in horse racing and breeding, the racecourse itself was a ramshackle affair. Most of the track was roughly defined by a handful of flags. The only rails were in the finishing straight, which also had a small red-and-white grandstand. Disconcertingly, we noticed that the rails were topped with a strand of barbed wire. What it was for, we couldn't imagine – perhaps it was a drastic measure to deter riders from falling off their mounts. The finishing line wasn't very sophisticated either – just a raised chair where a bloke, presumably the judge, sat and decided who'd won. A photo finish would undoubtedly have involved someone getting lucky with a Polaroid.

We bought some hot chips and started checking out the horseflesh. Twidkiwodm and I decided there was only one decent-looking horse among the pretty ordinary bunch being groomed for the next race. But neither of us had ever placed a bet with a bookmaker, so when we got to the betting ring we shuffled around trying to pluck up courage.

Everywhere we looked, the horse we'd chosen was 8–1. They seemed pretty good odds.

'You do it,' Twidkiwodm said.

'I can't. I don't know what to ask for. They'll laugh at me. Or they'll rip us off and then laugh at us.'

'No they won't. Why on earth would they do that?'

'Then you do it.'

The pot continued calling the kettle gutless until Heri showed up. He'd put a pound on the horse we thought would win. We asked him if he'd put a bet on for us. He refused – muttering something about it being against the law. I suspect he just liked to see us suffer. Still too timid to resolve the matter, we wandered over to what could be described as the horses' marshalling area (if you were being generous). It was up a bit of a hill from the finishing line, from where we could see the whole course.

The start itself was less than organised. There were no starting gates and there was a lot of shouting as the jockeys mounted and then jockeyed for position while grooms tugged at bridles trying to get the horses facing the right way. The tugging, shouting and milling went on until all of a sudden a man standing to the side raised a red flag then dipped it. The horses just broke away from the grooms and took off across the hills and dales of the track.

We had time to scamper down to the finish line for what we thought was the end of the race, but the horses charged by and started another lap. By this time we could see what the barbed wire was for. The crowd was so excited that they were climbing on the rails to get a better view, and it was only the barbs that stopped them leaning over and getting cleaned up as the field galloped past.

On the outside of the track, some of the crowd had ducked under the rail and were invading the course. All it would take was one wayward mount and they'd have been cashing in their betting slips at the pearly gates.

Around the field went again, hooves thundering, crowd shouting, the slap of the whips sounding clear and sharp as the horses charged for the finish. Our horse won easily.

'I told you you should have put some money on.'

'You could have done it just as easily.'

Heri grinned (slightly smugly, we felt) before

ducking off to collect his winnings.

As at the beginning of the race there was a mêlée of horses at the finish, but now they were joined by hundreds of excited spectators. The horses grew increasingly skittish and started dashing through the crowd, while a man shouted himself hoarse on a public address system: 'Ladies and gentlemen. Get back. For your own safety, get back. Get back, please.'

I don't know why he bothered. Even I had been in Ireland long enough to know no one would take a bit of notice. They were having too much fun.

7

HEADING NORTH

Compared to the previous day, breakfast the next morning was a subdued affair. We were leaving Dingle, which meant we had to say goodbye to Paul, Heri and Kobi. In the great travellers' tradition, we exchanged addresses and said they were welcome to visit whenever they wanted. And we meant it. Subsequently, and I don't know how it happened, we lost the address. I've rifled my notebooks, guidebooks and every place I can think of many times, but I've never been able to find it. Maybe one of them will read this and get in touch.

After the trouble we'd had getting to Dingle, we decided to take the most direct route to Tralee, which we had to pass through a second time now we were starting north. Paul and the kids dropped us in town on their way to see the beehive huts and the sights we'd seen a couple of days before. Although we knew what lay ahead of them, we couldn't help feeling that we were missing something.

The town was still pretty quiet as we walked past some of its 52 pubs. From the time we'd spent in some of them we knew that no matter which one you went into, you had every chance of getting a good pint of Guinness after a long day walking, cycling, windsurfing, playing with the fauna or going to the races. Or whatever else amused you.

'Hell of a nice town,' I said, as we shuffled along.

'Damn nice,' Twidkiwodm agreed.

People talk about places like Dingle becoming spoiled by tourism. It's certainly getting more crowded but that doesn't necessarily spell disaster. As someone who likes to zig when everyone else is zagging, I know you can always find 'the road less travelled'. Or at least a quiet corner, a snug in a pub perhaps, where you can settle back and talk about life's adventures.

We wandered along the Tralee road as a light Irish mist started to fall. Twidkiwodm went into a small shop to buy some barley sugar for our journey. When she came out she told me she'd had a bit of a yarn with the lady behind the counter. 'She had a nice expression for rain,' she said. '"The weather's gone soft."'

It got softer and softer as we walked to the edge of town, where we found a good hitching spot near a church. We could hear hymns being sung and there was a crowd of vehicles on the road and in the churchyard. If we didn't get a lift before the service ended, chances were a good Christian soul might help his fellow citizens.

We were still there, slightly damp, when people started pouring out of the church. Cars started rolling by. We were ignored. So much for loving your neighbour – presumably on the road it was 'Save yourself; hitchhikers be damned'. Soon the churchyard and the road were empty. There was just one car left, belonging to the priest. We watched him as he locked up the church, got in his car. Then he drove past us too.

'Barley sugar?' Twidkiwodm asked.

'Thanks.'

So… here we were again. Standing in the rain is one of the prices you pay for not having a car or not being on an organised tour. And you can also miss a lot of the sights. But there is an upside. You can find yourself with people like Paul or with the locals that tourists are usually dying to meet. And often it's the people tourists would run from who are the most interesting. In our circumstances, if such people were prepared to offer us a lift, we weren't about to argue. And that's what makes all the difference.

We persisted with our thumbs until a bloke in a delivery van finally took pity on us. To our good fortune he was going all the way to Tralee. And there's nothing like a ride that gets you well on your journey to lift your spirits. It also lets you enjoy the scenery rather than be an unwilling part of it.

'Ah yes, there's many hitchhikers on this road,' the bloke said. 'I like stoppin' for 'em when I can. I enjoy the company and ye meet people from all over the world.'

When we got to Tralee, he went out of his way to drop us at the right road to our next destination, Tarbert on the River Shannon. Another advantage of getting rides with the locals is that you don't get lost in the labyrinth of Irish roads. And knowing where you're going is particularly useful in a country where the road signs aren't terribly well attached to their poles. Often they seem to indicate wind direction rather than routes to towns.

HALF AN HOUR later we got a lift to the town of Listowel, halfway between Tralee and Tarbert. And no, once again in Tralee we didn't see any of the much-vaunted Roses thereof. What could they possibly be doing? The closest we got was a little girl who walked past us with her parents – a budding rose, perhaps.

Meanwhile, the man who gave us a ride tried to make up for our disappointment by telling us that Listowel was famous for its writers. 'There's hoondreds of 'em,' he said. In fact, the little town is supposed to be or have been home to at least sixty writers who'd written nearly 400 books. Exactly why it should be so blessed is anybody's guess. It didn't look any more or less inspiring than any other Irish town but perhaps it satisfied the two prerequisites for any artistic enclave: it's pleasant and the rents are cheap.

Our driver dropped us out the front of John B. Keane's pub and told us the eponymous proprietor was the most famous writer of the lot. Or maybe that was the reason Listowel was popular with writers: a fellow writer owned a pub.

We probably shouldn't have been surprised to find that the pub didn't stock any books. Beer? Wine? Spirits? No problem. The lady behind the counter did tell us there was a good bookshop just down the street, facing the town square. It wasn't far but along the way we still managed to see something that stopped us in our tracks. Across the street a man was carrying two shotguns, one broken over each arm, and a rifle slung over his shoulder; his chest was criss-crossed by ammunition belts, and another ammo belt looped around his waist. The headline flashed before my eyes: 'Shooting rampage in Listowel. Australian couple slain.' At that moment I noticed two Garda walking towards the brazen psychopath. I started looking for a shop we could duck into to take cover from the inevitable hail of lead. But no – the Garda walked straight past the gunman without batting an eyelid.

Somewhat unsettled, we found the bookshop and Twidkiwodm eventually bought a copy of John B. Keane's *The Bodhrán Makers* (a bodhrán is a small Irish drum). I rummaged around hoping to find some body armour, but the bookshop took its brief as literally as the pub did. Since we'd bought a copy of the book and the author's tavern was just down the street, we thought we might go back, have a Guinness and see if we could get the man himself to sign it. As it happened, on our return there was a man behind the counter talking with the woman who'd been there earlier. Apart from them, the place was empty. The man glanced at our backpacks and the paper bag from the bookshop, and wandered out the back.

'I bet that was him,' I said. 'Go on. Go after him.'

Twidkiwodm pushed the book at me and said, 'No. You're a writer. You ask him.'

Here we were again. We debated the issue until finally I took the book and fronted the bar. 'Two pints of Guinness, please,' I said. I put the book down in clear view. The dialogue was now supposed to go, 'Certainly sir. And I see you have a copy of *The Bodhrán Makers*, by John B. Keane. Actually, John's just out the back. Would you like me to go and see if he'll sign it for you?'

'Oh, would you? That would be wonderful.'

Instead, the woman poured the Guinness without a word. Damn. I took the drinks to the table where Twidkiwodm was sitting. She gave me hell. There wasn't even much pleasure to be had from my Guinness. It couldn't get the taste of sheepishness out of my mouth.

Finally, Twidkiwodm went over to the lady at the bar, who we were starting to suspect was John B.'s wife, and said, 'Look, if it isn't too much trouble, is there any chance that John's here and might sign this book for us, please?'

Mrs Keane narrowed her eyes. 'I think he may have left. Wait a moment and I'll go and see.'

She disappeared out the door after John B. We heard low voices muttering for a moment. We couldn't be sure if there was muffled laughter. Then the woman reappeared. 'I'm sorry,' she said. 'You've just missed him.'

We were defeated. However, I still have an image of two writers standing on either side of a wall too shy to meet face to face. OK. Maybe it was just one.

We left John B. Keane's and headed down the street, tails between our legs. But we hadn't gone ten paces when I stopped. 'Twidkiwodm,' I said. 'Give me that book.'

'Why? What for?'

'Don't argue,' I said firmly. 'Just give it to me.'

I rushed back to the bar and burst in the door.

Sure enough, there was John B. Keane, back behind the bar. A smile of self-congratulation was dying on his lips.

'Aha,' I cried, advancing on the cornered author. 'The game's up.'

Then I felt a hand tugging at my sleeve. 'Stop daydreaming.' Twidkiwodm was beside me; we were still out on the street. 'Come on.'

As for the book itself, I don't know anything about it because I never got to read it. After we left Ireland, Twidkiwodm took it to Spain and lent it to some bloke in Barcelona. She didn't get it back. It's probably one of those traveller's novels by now, going all over the world. Not that it would be hard to work out what it was about – making bodhráns, at a guess. And being Irish, it would involve crushing hardship. And yet, the people would endure.

GETTING A RIDE the fifteen kilometres from Listowel to Tarbert was easy. On the other hand, heading towards the Shannon was making us increasingly uneasy. This is because anyone who has read or seen *Angela's Ashes* will have come to the conclusion that the Shannon is Ireland's answer to Africa's ebola virus. The reason is that the young Frank McCourt spent part of his relentlessly miserable childhood in the town of Limerick, further up the Shannon. And while his family was living there, two of his brothers succumbed to pneumonia. McCourt blames the river.

It's probably fair to say that the Limerick tourism association isn't one of McCourt's biggest fans. Not after they read things like 'You're bound to have the cough when you live in Limerick because this is the capital city of the weak chest and the weak chest leads to consumption. If all the people that has [sic] consumption in Limerick were to die this would be a ghost town.' Nor should McCourt hold his tubercular breath for the keys to the city after a line such as 'He's far from the Shannon dampness that kills'.

I should, though, add a small note in McCourt's defence. Not long ago I was waiting for a plane in London when I noticed an Irish kid nearby who was frequently convulsed by a terrible barking cough. He and his dad boarded the flight being called for Limerick.

Luckily for us, the grim reaper had taken a break from blighting the Tarbert part of the Shannon. The town was bathed in warm late-afternoon sunshine as we booked into a hostel set on a hill overlooking the alleged River of Death. We planned to cross the mouth of the river by ferry the next morning so as to give ourselves a full day to hitchhike on the other side. We certainly didn't want to be near the Shannon without a lift as darkness fell. At night the lethal atmosphere would claim us for sure.

We dropped our gear and I went off to buy bread and milk. I noticed a shopkeeper chatting to one of her customers in Gaelic. As I browsed the shelves I eavesdropped, struck by how melodic the language was. It was almost as if they were reciting poetry. When I got to the counter, I was content to wait for the women to finish talking but the shopkeeper immediately broke off and started serving me, speaking in English. It must have been pretty obvious I wasn't a local. Then as she counted out my change, I suddenly had an idea. When she was done I took a deep breath and said, '*Go raibh maith aguth.*'

Hopefully I'd said 'Thank you' in Gaelic, not something like 'Your cow seems to have foot and mouth'. Anyway, the effect was sensational. Both women gaped. Then the shopkeeper eventually stammered out a 'You're welcome' in English. It may have been the first time a stranger had even tried to speak their language (or perhaps I *had* given her bad news about the cow). Mustering as much nonchalance as I could, I smiled, picked up my shopping and left. Behind me I could hear their tongues already flying (in Gaelic). It wasn't much, but thanks to Ciaran's dad, I'd got to speak it with the natives.

Later, over dinner at the hostel, we not only discovered that one of the other guests was a countryman but, more significantly, he told us he was a vet. This struck Twidkiwodm and I as potentially very convenient, because the next day marked more than a week since the stitches had been put in my hand. So it was time for them to come out.

'When you say vet,' I said as disingenuously as I could, 'are we talking about a fair degree of skill in, say, minor surgical procedures?'

'Involving animals, yes,' he said, probably suspicious already.

'So, if I had to get a couple of stitches out, say tomorrow, and wasn't likely to be in the vicinity of a hospital, someone of your calibre might be ideally placed to do the job?'

'I'm a vet, not a doctor,' he replied. He was following the logic, though not altogether willingly.

'Well, can you at least look at it and tell us what you think?' Twidkiwodm cajoled, this technique being one of her fortés.

He reluctantly agreed and I took off the bandage. Even I could tell it didn't look terribly flash. You didn't have to know about the rowing, cycling, windsurfing or dolphin-watching to see that.

The vet took one glance and said, 'I think you should show it to someone who's qualified.' What a puss.

The next morning, over breakfast, we gave him another chance. 'We've decided to take the stitches out anyway,' I said. 'But let's face it, you're a lot more qualified than us.'

'Look, I'm really sorry,' he replied. 'But you should see a doctor.'

'Oh, OK. Don't worry about it,' Twidkiwodm said. 'I'll do it myself.' She got out a Swiss army knife and put the blade into a pot of water on the stove to sterilise. I was impressed. It was almost like a real surgical procedure.

When Vetboy realised we were serious, it seemed to make him really nervous. 'Look,' he said. 'Wait. Can you wait ten minutes?'

He's finally cracked, we thought. 'Sure,' we chorused. Instead, it seems, he rapidly packed his belongings and fled the premises. Maybe he thought we'd sue him if things went wrong. Still, his lack of confidence did nothing to bolster mine.

'You do know what you're doing?' I asked Twidkiwodm.

'Of course. I was raised in the country. I looked after animals all the time.'

'And you've taken stitches out of some of them?'

'Well, no. Not exactly. But hey, how hard can it be?'

'Oh, for goodness sake.' I was starting to wish I was with Vetboy, speeding from the scene down some country lane.

'Don't be such a baby. Give me your hand and let's get this over with.'

'Wait a second,' I said, trying to buy time. 'If you had stitches, would you let me take them out?'

'Are you out of your mind?' she said.

She had a point. And the rest of the blade that was attached to it. So those readers of a squeamish disposition may want to skip a page… now.

Perhaps predictably, the operation fell a bit short of what you'd call a complete success. Actually, 'disaster' would be considerably more accurate. Our problems started with the choice of surgical equipment. The blade of the Swiss army knife was pretty sharp, but we hadn't counted on those stitches being such tough little blighters. So Twidkiwodm didn't so much cut through them as saw. When she did manage to get through the cords, we found that the wound hadn't really healed very well. Actually, it peeled open before our eyes. Alas, I don't know the correct medical term for yucky, but that's certainly how it looked.

'What if we use plasters to hold it together and you try to keep your hand straight as much as possible?' Twidkiwodm suggested.

'You mean tape it shut?'

'It's worth a try.' She was starting to look like she felt she should have listened to Vetboy. I wondered if that was sufficient cause to sue him, wherever he was. He probably had a duty of care to be more assertive.

Anyway, the plaster solution seemed to work reasonably well. The only drawback was that for the next couple of days I looked like I was marching everywhere. When I wasn't marching, I looked like I was about to give a left-handed salute.

HAVING DRESSED MY wounds, we prepared to cross the Styx (as we'd come to think of the Shannon). It was a long, bracing stroll from town to the dock, but the prospects for hitching once we got to the other side looked reasonably good. We counted 44 cars driving onto the ferry and they had plenty of time to check us out and come to the inevitable conclusion that we were two of the nicest people they could possibly give a lift to. And we badly needed a ride because the weather was deteriorating, threatening to spread its lethal Shannon dampness over all. Even so, the river had a sombre majesty that morning. On both shores there were large, looming power stations. Heavy dark clouds floated low over the broad expanse of leaden water. As the ferry crawled slowly forward, butting into the choppy waves and current, there was a definite grandeur in the scene.

No one offered us a lift while we were on the ferry, so we made sure we were first off when we got to the Killimer side. I noticed a few spits of rain as the cars rolled off and we stuck out our hopeful thumbs. When the last car drove past us and the ferry pulled away from the shore, we found ourselves alone – just two more pieces of refuse among the flotsam and jetsam strewn along that solitary shore (well, there was a café but it rather spoils the image).

It started to rain. We started to walk. We headed for what we hoped was the centre of Killimer, thinking that if the rain didn't stop we'd find shelter there. The ferry dock was on a side-road and when we got to the main road we discovered that Killimer was just a scattering of houses, none of which had so much as a verandah to huddle under. There was no traffic at all. As the rain grew heavier, the prospect of perishing reared its ugly head. Even if someone came along, we were now so wet that the chances of them stopping to pick us up were practically nil. I could see the headline: 'Shannon damp claims two more! Garda baffled by victim's death salute.'

Then, in the distance, we heard a car. A little sedan came around a corner at speed, too fast to stop, and I said 'Not a chance.' Still, I stuck out my thumb just in case.

The driver immediately slammed on the brakes and pulled up right in front of us. Then he leaned across and threw open the passenger door. He was an extremely presentable fellow of around fifty, in tweeds and a tie.

'What are y' doin' out in this terrible weather?'

he shouted at us. 'You'll catch yer dett. Get in! Quickly now.'

God bless the Irish. God bless them, every one.

It didn't bother Declan at all that we were saturated or that we were rapidly drenching the interior of his car. He drove straight to the town of Kilrush, pointed out a café and shouted at us some more. 'Now get in dere. They've a warm fire and good coffee. Go on, get along now.' Feeling like naughty children, we did as we were told.

As we slowly turned in front of the fire, we revised our plans. We had been hoping to head for the Cliffs of Moher, which were on the coast about sixty kilometres north. The problem was that in that direction there was a maze of roads and towns that would make hitchhiking difficult. And it was still raining. While we might meet another Declan, we very well might not.

Also near the Cliffs were the towns of Lisdoonvarna and Doolin, whose pubs, we'd been told, had the best Irish music anywhere. We'd had no reports on the quality of the Guinness, but we had been subjected to a drunken Irish girl who sat in The Laurels in Killarney one night singing, 'Oooh Lisdoonvarna. Lisdoon, Lisdoon, Lisdoon,

Lisdoonvarna' over and over until she finally fell asleep. Despite this we wanted to go there and experience some traditional Irish music, even though Pat and Ciaran hadn't rated it highly on their must-see list. 'We're not mooch into dat diddly-di-di music,' they said.

'What sort of music are you into?'

'U2.' Irish. Sort of.

While Twidkiwodm and I debated what to do, we noticed a bus pulled up in the main street. Its sign said it was going to Ennis: this wasn't quite on the route to Lisdoonvarna, Doolin and the Cliffs, but it was in the right direction if you interpreted the expression fairly broadly.

Buses and timetables being something of a novelty in this part of the world, I went out and asked the driver if he was really going to Ennis.

'Dat's roit,' he said, 'oonless dat soign on de front dere is wrong.'

'And when might you be leaving?'

'Aah now. I'll be goin' when all me passengers get here.'

Of course. How stupid of me.

'I'd say dey'll be about half an hour,' he added.

'Thanks. My friend and I would like to come too.

176

Will we see you in half an hour?'

'No trooble at all. Oi've plenty of room,' he said. 'Ond if ye don't moind me askin', what part of the world would ye be from?'

'Australia,' I told him. 'Sydney.'

'Australia is it? Sure yer a terrible long way from home.'

'I wouldn't want to walk it.'

'There's no need,' he said, giving me an odd look. 'Dey've aeroplanes now. Anyway, I'll see ye when ye coom back.'

I went to the café and told Twidkiwodm the score. 'It's leaving in half an hour, give or take. If it's still raining then, I think we should go to Ennis.'

As the time passed, we watched passengers trickle up to the bus and climb aboard. The rain was still coming down when we ran across the square and got on too. The bus was half full – old men and women with string bags, mothers with small children quietly talking among themselves. Eventually, the arrival of another passenger seemed to be the signal for the driver to start the engine and say 'Roit. We'll be off.'

Just before he started moving, though, he turned to his passengers and pointed at us. 'Now, d'ye see dat yoong fella and dat yoong woman dere. Dey've coom all the way from Australia, would ye believe? And now, dere going to Ennis.' All the other passengers turned around to take in the novelty of us. Some smiled. Some just stared.

The bus trundled out into the countryside. Actually, dawdled may be a better description, if a bus is capable of such a thing. The driver seemed to have a proclivity for stopping at random. It was only when he did it for the third time that we started to realise how the bus service worked: the emphasis was on 'service'. Whenever the bus stopped we'd all sit there for a little while, until out of the landscape a person would appear and climb aboard. They'd exchange a greeting with the driver and the other passengers, and then we were off again. The driver was stopping because he knew who he was going to pick up. If they were late walking down the lanes to the main road, and some were old and slow, he'd wait for them to turn up. Perhaps that was why the bus driver had pointed us out: in a place where everyone was known to everyone else, we had to be accounted for.

By the time we got to Ennis, the weather was breaking and once again we were faced with a decision about which way to go. I'd been looking at the guidebook and realised that not far away from Ennis is Craggaunowen, where Tim Severin's leather boat is kept. But it was about twenty kilometres in the opposite direction from the Cliffs. We weighed our options. On the one hand we had the Cliffs of Moher, Lisdoonvarna, Doolin and, as we'd also read in our guidebook, the wild limestone-slabbed country of the Burren. On the other hand we had a leather boat.

It was a tough choice. That boat had taken me on a voyage across the Atlantic, up to the Faroe Islands, on to Iceland, then down the Greenland coast. I wanted to see where they'd stitched the leather hull after it had been holed by ice. I wanted to see the boat which had established how it was entirely possible that St Brendan had journeyed to America 1,500 years ago. Twidkiwodm didn't.

If we'd had a car, we could have seen both. But then, as it often does, fate made the decision for us. While we were still working out the right road to either destination, a young guy pulled up beside us and leaned across to the passenger side.

'Where ye goin'?' he shouted to us.

We hesitated for a moment, so he said 'I'm headed for Doolin. I can drop ye on the road to

Lisdoonvarna if that's where yer bound.' We had a lift to Doolin and points west. We didn't have one to the Brendan boat and sundries. So of course we piled into the little car.

Pat (yes, another one) was a barman in one of the pubs in Doolin, on his way to work. He soon convinced us it was every bit as good there as it was in Lisdoonvarna and it was closer to the Cliffs of Moher.

'Sure dere not very far,' he. 'If oive toim I'll show em to ye.'

It turned out he was going to Australia for an extended holiday once the Irish summer season was over. 'I taut ye moit be Aussies when I saw yer backpacks,' he said. 'I can't wait to get out of this place. It's so depressin' in winter. It's cold and dark fer moonths.'

His ambition when he got there was to spend several weeks soaking up the sun on the beach at Bondi. And he didn't expect to be lonely. He told us there were so many Irish people there it was referred to as County Bondi.

Pat ended up taking us to the Cliffs. From there it was possible to walk to Doolin and we might have done so if we hadn't had our packs, Pat waiting for us and rain blowing sideways off the Atlantic Ocean. Under the circumstances, we made our visit quick. Even without the breathtakingly sharp wind and cold, we would have been gasping in awe. As the rain and mist blew straight up the sheer black faces of the cliffs, we joined the legion of determined souls, wrapped in wet-weather gear, leaning into the gale to peer down at the ocean crashing against the shore far below. The crags themselves were dotted with nesting seabirds, while others soared and swept across the rocky face, a view that had vertigo-sufferers such as myself hankering for the carpark.

In typical Irish fashion there was a small watchtower (O'Brien's Tower) perched on one of the most exposed sections of cliff. The path leading up to it followed steps made from large sheets of local slate, presumably the material the cliffs were composed of. All around there were signs warning people not to venture too near to the edge, but they were hard to see because of all the people who'd climbed over the railings to get their photos taken. Call me a worrier but I could already hear the slide-show commentary: 'This is where Harold was standing when he slipped. This is Harold dashed to pieces on the rocks below. And this is a shot from half-way down, after Mabel slipped while she was taking the photo of Harold.' That's vertigo for you.

Doolin wasn't so much a town as a close affiliation of houses, hostels, B&Bs and pubs. Pat dropped us at a hostel after pointing out the pub where he worked, McGann's. We got beds for the night, dropped our bags on them and went for a stroll down to the waterside where there was a small port for boats that serviced the nearby Aran Islands. There was a pub in the lower town too, O'Connor's, where we nipped in for a quick pint before heading up to see Pat. We'd decided to eat dinner at McGann's and we weren't disappointed. We lashed out on two courses, a delicious chowder and a tomato and carrot soup, followed by baked salmon for Twidkiwodm and spicy chicken for me, both with the usual mountains of potato, carrots and cabbage. While the spicy chicken was good, I ended up wishing I'd had the salmon. There's no doubt that if you're going to eat anything in Ireland, it has to be salmon. Especially with a pint of Guinness.

The main attraction at McGann's, though, was the music. As the pub grew increasingly crowded, a handful of people eventually detached themselves from the bar and congregated around a table in the corner. They fiddled with various instruments for quite some time, adjusting bodhráns, flutes, banjos, guitars and a bass before launching into a range of songs that were remarkably similar to the ones we'd heard in O'Donoghue's, back in Dublin. The only real difference was the circle of tourists that surrounded the musicians with video cameras. The locals thronged the bar and ignored the band until they stopped for a break and went back to drinking.

We sat back from the band in the disputed territory between locals and tourists. After a while, some young locals asked if we'd share our table. We said we didn't mind, although we might have thought differently if we'd known they'd spend most of their time trying to work out why they couldn't make a call on their mobile phone. It was a clash of old and new, which the old won hands down – the music went late into the night without either batteries or network coverage. It even outlasted the batteries on most of the video cameras, so their owners were forced, one by one, to put them away and actually sit and listen.

STANDING AT THE window of the hostel the next morning, our bags packed, I watched hail clatter down outside. It didn't look good for hitchhiking through the Burren. We were just starting to think of another day in Doolin or a quick run over to Lisdoonvarna when there was a break in the brooding sky. We got our thumbs out.

As luck would have it, we didn't have to wait long for a lift from a young German couple who were heading up through the Burren to Ballyvaughan, on the edge of Galway Bay. Their route couldn't have been better as far as we were concerned – up through Lisdoonvarna and on past the Poulnabrone Dolmen, in the heart of the Burren itself.

Lisdoonvarna's main claim to fame is that it's the site of an annual bachelor festival. This used to be a local ritual for finding partners but these days it's more of a tourist attraction. We'd already missed the event, somewhat to our disappointment as Twidkiwodm and I could still be said to be on the hunt in the partner stakes. And we didn't even get to see much of the town, as our companions were more keen to 'zee ze vild Burren'.

We continued on with them, keeping a sharp eye out for signs to the Poulnabrone Dolmen. It turned out to be on the southern edge of the Burren, which starts abruptly just to the north of Lisdoonvarna. One moment you're driving through lush green fields, then the road climbs a steep rise and suddenly you're negotiating fields of rocks. As one of Cromwell's men famously put it, in the Burren there wasn't 'water enough to drown a man, nor a tree to hang him, nor soil enough to bury him'.

And yet the Burren only appears to be barren. At first glance it's nothing more than bare limestone slabs split by long deep cracks, but the region once supported a much larger population and there are literally thousands of ancient forts, tombs and monuments. Clearing the trees meant the shallow soil quickly washed away, exposing the limestone beneath: it has become, in effect, a high-rainfall desert. But it's still one of the most diverse eco-systems in Europe, with a huge range of plants sprouting in every available niche and patch of soil.

Despite or because of this, the Burren is a striking place. And one of the most striking things in it is the Poulnabrone Dolmen, the region's signature megalithic site. It's made up of four large slabs of stone upended to support a huge slab roof. It might be even more striking if it were somewhere other than in the middle of a rocky paddock surrounded by cows. I may have said it before, but the Irish do have a pretty casual attitude to their ancient sites.

Perhaps the feeling is that if something has been there for thousands of years already and nothing has happened to it, why start worrying now?

There was no attendant at the Dolmen, just a sign requesting a donation for the farmer whose land it was on. We tossed a couple of coins into the bucket, then rock-hopped and cowpat-dodged our way to the monument. It may have been the lichen, or perhaps it was the ponderous size of the slabs, but it not only looked old, it felt old. Whoever built it sure knew their stuff. The Dolmen wasn't falling down, coming apart or passing its use-by date: it was just weathering, and that in itself was an art.

WE CONTINUED NORTH, stopping for sights and photos along the way, such as a megalithic tomb on a property that had a friendly sign saying 'KEEP OUT'. We took our chances, though the tomb wasn't as impressive as the Dolmen. But nearby there was a monument to the discovery of a gold collar (called a torc) in the vicinity in 1932, one of the many torcs we'd seen at the National Museum in Dublin.

As we headed towards Ballyvaughan, we were treated to a dark cloudburst sweeping in over the Burren's silver-grey rocky plateau. The effect was far more dramatic than anything sunny skies could ever hope to match and as the rain came down we were grateful we were in a car. Fortunately, the storm had passed by the time our German companions dropped us in the centre of Ballyvaughan. After a sandwich in a café, we headed out towards the town's Burren interpretive centre (the 'Burren Exposure' – which could well be an oxymoron). It was a bit of a walk and as we wandered along, taking in the views of the harbour and Galway Bay, we tried to thumb a ride. We really should have gone to the 'Burren Exposure', but along the way we got yet another offer we thought we couldn't refuse – a lift to Galway in a farmer's truck. Little did we know.

'There's too mooch joonk in the cab,' the farmer said. 'D'ye moind roidin' in de back dere?'

A lift was a lift.

'Cloimb in den,' he said. 'Ye moit be more coomfortable if ye pull dat tarpaulin over ye both to break de wind.'

We found a place for ourselves among the bits of farm machinery, wooden boxes, sacks of potatoes, and assorted odds and ends. Then with an 'Are ye roit den?' from him and a wave from us, we took off. It was then that we discovered we'd booked a one-way ticket to hell. It wasn't just that we were sitting on the hard metal floor of the truck tray. It wasn't that the road was pocked with jarring potholes. It was that as well as all this, while most of the truck was slowly giving up the ghost, the suspension had already gone to a better place. Pretty soon we were wishing we were with it – we were in absolute butt-bruising agony.

So did we complain? Not for a second. Instead, we emulated the Irish approach to hardship. We tried to endure. When at last we got to Galway, we climbed gingerly out of the truck, politely thanked the farmer as sincerely as we could and staggered off doing the odd walk of people with no buttocks.

To add to our woes, we didn't know there was a music festival underway. It didn't take us long to find out, though, as we rang around every hostel and were told they were all full. As we grew increasingly desperate, one of them suggested we try the Tourist Office and stay at a B&B. The office, in the centre of town, was easy to find – there was a stream of people heading in its direction. Inside, we discovered a scene of flustered chaos. It was a bit like the operations room for a major military action, with some people working the phones and other people rushing back and forth with little slips of paper. Busiest of all were a couple of young women at the front counter taking down details from the crowd of people pushing towards them.

'How many are you? Do you mind sharing? What price range? Do you mind if you're a little way out of town? Now don't worry, there's still plenty of rooms about. It'll take joost a little while. Next please.' There was no 'Did ye never think to book ahead on this our busiest noit of the year, ye daft foreign eejit.' Though as more and more people kept coming in, they had to be thinking it.

While we waited our turn, we noticed a few other backpackers waiting as well. One was a girl we recognised from Dingle, and there were two young guys muttering to themselves in American accents. We made eye contact, half-smiled, resisted the urge to lunge at the counter to make sure we got the last room left in Galway. Then the doors opened again and the two Italians from Dingle – Marco and Michele – walked in. As soon as they saw us, their faces lit up: 'Evans! Michelle! How are you?'

'All the better for seeing you. How are ya?'

'Ooh. Is difficult. We are now searching for place to slip.'

'Do you want to try and get a place with us?' Twidkiwodm suggested.

'Oh yes, this is good.' They were relieved not to have to negotiate accommodation with their patchy English.

'It'll be a little more expensive than a hostel. Is that OK?'

'Yes, yes, we understand. Is OK for us.'

The boys piled their backpacks with ours, out of the way against a wall. They minded them while Twidkiwodm and I queued at the counter. Then I glanced at the girl from Dingle, who was on her own. She'd seen the whole exchange with the boys and looked a bit lost. Well, it was turning into a party. What was one more? 'Hi, if we can organise it, do you want to join us?'

She didn't hesitate. 'Yes please. I vould like zis very much.'

Her name was Ulrike. From Germany. She shook hands with us. We introduced ourselves and the boys.

Then the two young American guys piped up. 'Aah, hi there,' they said. 'Can we come too?' Glen and John waited with the others while Twidkiwodm and I breasted the counter. A young woman with short dark hair and slightly pink cheeks tried to smile while she said 'Is it joost the two?'

As she started to note it down, I cleared my throat. 'Er... no. Actually, there's seven of us.' The woman's head swivelled up from the notepad. She didn't say anything, but a small twitch of one eye screamed 'You have got to be jokin'!'

'We could be four and three,' I added as a concession. 'If seven isn't possible.'

If you think about it, booking one place for seven is a lot less trouble than booking seven places for one. But I'm pretty sure the woman wasn't thinking about it. Instead, she took a very, very deep breath, glanced over my shoulder at the crowd of people looking at her hopefully from the other side of the room, and lied. 'No problem. D'ye moind sharin'?'

We didn't.

'Proice range?'

'As cheap as possible.'

'D'ye moind if it's out of town a way?'

'We're on foot. Something within walking distance would be better.'

'Would a short roid in a taxi be alroit? It wouldn't cost ye mooch.'

For a moment I considered quibbling. Then I noticed the woman's eye twitch again. Not quibbling

191

looked a safer option. 'Yes, that'll be fine.'

'Roit then,' she said. 'It won't be long.'

She pulled off a great deal. If we shared, we could get two rooms in a nearby B&B for the standard price of two doubles, but split it seven ways. It worked out only a couple of pounds more than a hostel. We'd need taxis to get there with our backpacks, but when we were unencumbered it would be an easy walk back to town along the shore of Galway Bay.

DESPITE CONSIDERABLE COMPLAINING from me, Twidkiwodm decided we'd walk with our packs anyway, to save money. It wasn't the distance I minded, it was just that I was carrying her heavy backpack and it kept slipping down because I still had no arse. So our little band of travellers hiked along. We crossed a bridge over the torrent that is the River Corrib and followed it a short distance downstream to where the rush of water was swallowed, without a ripple, by Galway Bay. While we kept an eye out for the B&B, we caught up on our adventures.

Marco and Michele had been to Limerick (and lived) and to Bunratty Castle. 'We liking thissa monument verrrry much,' Marco told us with his fabulous accent. He had the ability to rrrrroll his rrrrrrs constantly, from somewherrrrre down at the back of his thrrrrrroat. Of course, it could have been the first sign of consumption.

When we got to our accommodation we quickly realised it was less a B&B and more somebody's home. The woman of the house was busy kicking a couple of kids out of their bedrooms and cramming them in with several others behind a sliding door off the lounge.

'Oh no, it's no trooble at all,' our landlady said as we apologised for creating havoc by arriving practically unannounced.

I started to suspect her children took a different view when one of the girls stuck her tongue out at Twidkiwodm. That's nothing, I was tempted to tell her: in Indonesia a little girl tried to put a curse on Twidkiwodm because she wouldn't buy some pottery. Then out of the blue a policeman appeared and belted the kid with a stick. Ever since, I've thought twice about cursing Twidkiwodm.

While the landlady made the cups of tea she insisted we have, we worked out the sleeping arrangements. There were two rooms, each with a double bed and a single. I suggested it should be girls in one room, the one overlooking Galway Bay, and boys in the other.

'Don't be ridiculous. Five in one room? Two in the other?' Twidkiwodm overruled me. 'Ulrike won't mind if you and I share the double bed. If you can behave.'

This meant that in the other room only one of the boys would have to sleep on the floor. There was a brief period of macho foot-shuffling while we decided which two boys would share the double bed in their room and who would get a foam mattress on the floor. Of the two nationalities, the Americans looked the more rugged outdoor types. Neither of the Italians looked like they'd ever slept anywhere that didn't have a roof. And since Italian men are prepared to kiss in public, it was decided they would mind least if they had to share a double bed.

Of course, having expressed a preference to sleeping separately from Twidkiwodm, a certain amount of interest was aroused among the boys. 'Tell me, Evans,' Michele said. 'Is rude I ask? Issa Michelle yorra girlfriend?'

'Sort of,' I replied.

'Sorry. I not know sort of.'

'That's OK. Do you know "friends"?'

194

'Yes. I know this word.'

'Good. Do you know "lover"?'

'Love. Yes, this too.'

'Well. It's a bit of both. Sometimes friends. Sometimes lovers. Understand?'

He scrunched up his face, then said 'No. Err, you see Marco and me. We are friend. And friend for long time is love. Si? But... ' he shrugged and grinned, 'I sink Marco iss not girlfriend.'

The question of my relationship with Twidkiwodm had cropped up during our travels from time to time. I'd found it easier to be vague about it ever since an American woman succeeded in her attempts to mine me for details. 'How much do you care about her?' she'd asked.

'A lot,' I'd answered, trying to empty my pint so I'd have an excuse to get away.

'Yes but how much?'

'Well,' I said, 'sometimes I think beyond if we got married to what it would be like if we had kids. And I think that any children of hers would be lucky to have her for a mother. She has so many interests that I think she'd share all kinds of wonderful things with them.'

The American woman almost burst into tears.

'That's the most beautiful thing I have ever heard,' she said.

I shrugged. 'It's alright.'

With that, my inquisitor got up and walked down to the other end of the table and told Twidkiwodm what I'd said. I could do nothing but sit there with a hand over my eyes, shaking my head in disbelief. When I looked up, Twidkiwodm was giving me the 'I will deal with you later' look.

When the landlady came back with the tea, she was full of information on Galway and its surrounds, which she proceeded to dispense at considerable length. We got all the stuff about it being a university town with a colourful history, and about the Aran Islands just offshore, where the jumpers come from. 'I'm sure you're knowin' about our music festival,' she said.

'We do now.'

'Well, I expect you'll be lookin' for a place where you can enjoy some of our traditional Irish music,' she continued, without missing a beat.

'As a matter of fact, yes we are.'

'Well, I'm told the An Pucan is quite good, ' she said. 'They say soom of the best musicians are to be found dere.'

'Have you been there yourself?' Twidkiwodm asked the questions others wouldn't dare touch.

'Well, I won't say as I haven't but it's not often you'll catch me in a place like dat. You're yoong though. I'm sure you'll be enjoying the craic dere soon enough. And don't be wooryin' about when ye coom home. Me hoosband'll see ye in. He's not a good one for sleepin'.'

As I understood it, our host was giving us permission to listen to wild Irish music until the wee small hours, drink copious amounts of Guinness, stagger home in our own personal windstorms and then expect to be put to bed where we'd lapse into comas face-down in puddles of our own drool until morning. Which, in a nutshell, is what we did.

I DON'T KNOW the exact translation of An Pucan, but in essence it stands for fiddle and bodhrán, tin whistle and voice, ballad and reel. The pub was packed with people – most of them rowdy and incredibly social. Under the circumstances, they had to be. It was so crowded that if you wanted to talk it was easier to do it with the people around you rather than squeeze your way back to your friends.

At one point I looked across the room and saw Ulrike, Glen and John standing together and grinning. Then I realised they weren't actually doing anything like talking or dancing. They were just... enjoying themselves.

'I see you're drinkin' the Guinness,' an Irish bloke next to me shouted in my ear.

'It's great,' I said. 'Moother's milk.' It was hard not to fall into the accent.

'Oh, this isn't bad,' my companion said, 'but there's a place a little way out of town where it's the best.'

'Near here?'

'D'ye know Connemara?'

I had a vague idea it was an expanse of windswept mountains west of Galway. 'What's so special about it?'

'Aah now. It's because of de water dey use to wash out de loins.'

I guessed he meant the tubes between keg and tap. Anyway, I hoped he did.

'De water dey use cooms from a stream that roons near the place. Sure it's the purest water in all Oirland. So after dey've cleaned the loins, all your tastin' is the Guinness, nootin' else.'

He then proceeded to explain where this fabled place actually was. It involved several roads with Gaelic names, others with route numbers, and endless lists of left-hand and right-hand. A better way of locating the place would have been to find a wild goose, take it to the vicinity of the pub and pursue it until it collapsed from exhaustion. When we'd established that the poor bird had indeed expired we'd raise our eyes and the pub would be before us in all its glory.

My man also said that 'If yer looky, you'll even be foindin' the poteen.'

'We already have,' I confessed. 'We drank some and lived.'

'Have you now,' he said, and his face darkened. 'Ye should be careful. Dat stoof will take your soit.'

Hadn't I heard that before?

When I asked him about a pub in Galway that still served Guinness in jugs, he looked at me like I was a fool. 'Soomwoon's pullin' yer leg,' he said.

He could talk. He'd just told me where to find the purest loins in Ireland.

Introducing the Italians to Guinness was a lot of fun, too. Generally speaking they are a highly expressive race of people, able to transmit a great deal of information with a multitude of facial expressions and hand gestures alone. This is especially the case when describing things for which there aren't actually any words, such as taste – as in, the taste of Guinness. We bought them a pint each and said 'Now, no matter what, you have to drink all of this.' They naïvely agreed.

Marco was first. He took a sip and a quick swallow. Obviously he immediately regretted it. His dark eyes actually ballooned, and, in the middle of his pale face and jet-black curly hair, they looked like bowling balls. As the liquid made its way down his throat, his face gradually compressed. Eventually, he was frowning so hard his knitted eyebrows looked like they'd make a sweater. Meanwhile, the knuckles on the hand that was holding his pint had gone white. His free hand was making jerky little circles in the air, like a windmill. At one point I'm sure he used sign language for SOS.

Michele reacted differently. Twidkiwodm suggested he roll the Guinness around his mouth 'to savour the flavour'. What followed was a near-fatal battle with the urge to spit. His hand clawed at the air as his tongue presumably did the same to the liquid that lay upon it. Watching him try to swallow was even more entertaining. It looked like he was trying to force the drink to the back of his throat where he could then think of some way to actually get it down. The Italians are a great football nation and I think Michele's tonsils may have been great goalies. It seemed to take him several shots before he got the Guinness past them. When he finally did, his mouth fell open and he hunched forward, head turning from side to side, trying to wipe his tongue on the air: 'Gaaaaa... gaaaaa...'

He sounded like a baby, which may be why they called Guinness mother's milk.

'So fellas,' I said chirpily. 'It's great stuff isn't it? Have some more.'

'No, Evans,' Michele moaned. 'I don like.'

'Is mistake,' Marco agreed. 'We cannot drink. We buy something else.'

It took a considerable amount of persuasion to get them to drink those first pints. But in the atmosphere of the An Pucan, it took considerably less to get them to have another.

WHEN TUESDAY DAWNED, a bright sun rose into a sky that was full of promise for a glorious day. The birds sang with a pure voice and all those who heard them felt good to be alive. Or so we were told when we got up for breakfast a couple of hours later.

Perhaps it was the weather, but even the landlady's kids were friendly. Or perhaps it was because they knew we were leaving. Not that they were getting their rooms back – we had to go because there was a prior booking. Rather than face another trial by accommodation, we decided to sightsee in the morning and then head off somewhere quieter. Exactly where, we weren't sure, especially after Marco and Michele explained that they had a problem.

'Evans, Michelle,' they said. 'We are enjoy your company very much. We would like to come with you but we have this thing, rail pass. We can only go where there is station for train.'

They liked us? Even after the Guinness? But it meant we had to find somewhere good on a train line. I was tempted to scour Connemara in search of the best Guinness (or Galway, for that matter, having not given up on the Stone Jug Pub) but we started looking at maps. We were forgetting the landlady, who quickly came to the rescue. 'Is it north you're heading?'

It was, except for Glen and John who were anticlockwise travellers, heading south. 'Then it'll be

Westport you'll be wantin'. Loovely place and a stone's throw from Croagh Patrick.'

'Crow who?'

'Ye don't know about Croagh Patrick. It's only the holiest mountain in all Ireland.'

ONCE AGAIN, IGNORANCE was about to be bliss.

THE HOLY MOUNTAIN

There's a body of opinion that there's nothing like the smell of napalm in the morning. However, as our platoon shouldered backpacks and moved out from the B&B, we had the scent of adventure as an alternative. Our operation was well planned. Accommodation organised in Westport: check (thanks to the landlady). Route to train station explained: check. Route to bus station (for Ulrike, Twidkiwodm and me, because it was cheaper than the train): check. Objective: Croagh Patrick (aka the Holy Mountain).

While we probed the narrow lanes that crossed and followed the canals of Galway town, Michele alternated between whistling what sounded like Scarlatti and singing songs in Italian. It wasn't so much *Apocalypse Now* as allegro pronto. From time to time, he'd break off to say 'Evans, what is mean this?', point to a street sign or ask about some odd expression he'd heard in English, and I'd try to explain. When he was satisfied, he started whistling again.

We were standing at an intersection waiting for the lights to change when I happened to look up and down the street, just to check things out. A woman beside me said, 'Are ye lost?'

'No, thanks,' I replied. 'We're just crossing the street.'

'And where would ye be goin'?'

'To the cathedral just down the street there.' It had a reputation as Ireland's ugliest, but I didn't like to tell the woman that.

'God bless ye. Are ye goin' to chorch?'

'No, just to have a look.'

'You've no need. It's a bloody catastrophe.'

'Just a quick look,' I amended.

She looked at me and realised I was determined. 'Suit yerself,' she said. 'Enjoy your day.'

As a building the cathedral was full of references to other times and events. It looked better from a distance, looming above the fast-flowing river. I made a note of its location, though, in case we ever had to call in an air strike.

LATER THAT MORNING our squad broke up and took various personnel carriers between Galway and Westport. Twidkiwodm, Ulrike and I were on the bus. With us, apart from the usual locals, was a young woman from America who was very nervous. We soon discovered, because she told everyone aboard, that she'd booked a farm stay, a traditional cottage experience somewhere along the route. But exactly where, she wasn't sure.

Perhaps it was beside the pub that poured the perfect Guinness. We knew she was in trouble when we realised that even the indigenes didn't seem to know where she was talking about. Not that they admitted it. Instead they offered conflicting suggestions and comments like 'Oi tink oive hoard of it', which made it clear they hadn't. And the weather had gone soft again. If she got it wrong she'd be stuck in the middle of nowhere, in the rain, with hours to wait until the next bus.

The road we were on only added to the confusion. As we'd already observed, the term 'road' is used in a rather cavalier fashion in Ireland. When you're in little more than a country lane weaving back and forth around the dry-stacked stone walls that divide the fields, it would be more accurate to say 'meander'. The road also sprouted countless side-roads in a confusion of lanes.

'If only she'd planned her operation as thoroughly as we did ours,' I said.

'What on earth are you going on about?' Twidkiwodm replied, with more than a hint of insubordination. I decided to let it go – this time.

For the hopeful farm-stayer, trying to locate a particular cottage among dozens of tumble-down dwellings was like trying to find a needle in a haystack. Several times she was sure she'd found it, but just as she was getting off the bus she lost her nerve. Another time, the bus driver said 'No, dat couldn't be it'. And after he'd continued a little way he said 'I'm sure dat wasn't it.' Eventually she shouted at the driver to stop. He obediently hit the brakes. She hesitated for a moment, looking at her woefully inadequate map, then without a word leapt off into the wilds of Ireland.

'Well, good luck to ye,' the driver said, and we all knew he meant it.

As we rolled on, Twidkiwodm and I listened to the two old men in the seat in front of us who were talking quietly to each other. We could hear the conversation clearly but couldn't understand a word of it. 'They're speaking Gaelic,' I whispered to Twidkiwodm. 'We must be in another Gaeltacht.'

We continued eavesdropping, enjoying the melodious, deep-voiced timbre of their exchange. Then with a shock we looked at each other. 'It's English!' But it was unlike any English we'd ever heard: the accent was so thick it was almost impossible to understand, and there was such a rhythm to it that they were all but singing. We could only imagine what they were talking about – fields, perhaps, and the price of cattle and the slow turn of seasons. Timeless things, we hoped. Then again they may have been saying 'Oim in trooble. The wife said if I forgot the toothpaste again I needn't bother coomin' back.'

The bus wove on between the fields, from time to time giving us glimpses of a distant pyramid-shaped mountain. It could have been any one of a thousand small peaks (or one of the 12 famous 'bens' of Connemara), but as we got closer it came to dominate the skyline and we hoped it was our destination, Croagh Patrick. Having not had much experience of holy mountains, I wasn't sure, but it certainly had what felt like the right aura.

WHEN WE ARRIVED in Westport, we quickly found out both that this was our mountain and that the woman at the B&B in Galway really knew her stuff. The Granary Hostel, on the road to Croagh Patrick, was a rustic place, to put it mildly. Rough wooden tables, bare wood floors, exposed beams supporting the floors above – yet cosy. It was a converted grain store, the conversion mainly comprising the removal of the grain and the installation of some beds.

As the weather was starting to alternate between soft and sunny, and Marco and Michele hadn't arrived, we went for a stroll around the nearby lanes and fields. We especially wanted to have a look at Westport House, the seat of the Earls of Altamont, who have turned the estate, built between 1730 and 1778, into a kind of theme park. The house, zoo and other attractions cost money to visit, but it was free to wander the grounds and so we took the road less charged for.

We had much of the garden to ourselves. Laid out in Anglo-Italian style, it was full of perfume that hung thickly in the warm afternoon air. Eventually the gardens gave way to fields, where the horses that hauled carts of tourists around had been turned out for the day. Most had a look that said 'If one more tourist tries to pat me, so help me, I'll whinny.' One of them had propped itself on its bottom with its hind legs sticking out straight. In that ungainly position it was slowly licking its back hooves – the picture of an exhausted quadruped.

Back at the Granary, not only had Marco and Michele arrived, but Horst and Michael, the German guys from the hostel in Killarney, had also turned up. When they heard of our plans for the next day, they immediately enlisted in our craic squad. Once again, we were a party of seven.

Our guidebook told us that one of the pubs in town was famous for its Irish music – Matt Molloy's, Matt being the flautist from The Chieftains. It could have been some residual issues I was having with the John B. Keane incident, but the idea of going somewhere that was famous for being owned by someone famous just didn't appeal. It might be like going to those café chains owned by movie stars or supermodels – you never know when Naomi Campbell or Liz Hurley is going to walk over and say 'Excuse me, aren't you Evan McHugh?' And you have to say 'Yes, but please respect my privacy.'

Instead, we went to a pub the guidebook was reduced to saying was quite nice (the subtext being: Didn't we just tell you to go to Matt Molloy's? What's wrong with you?). Hoban's faced the Octagon at the top of the main street. It really was an octagon, too, not like the usual square of other towns. Those wacky Westportians.

In the middle of the Octagon they also had a statue of St Patrick, with a few lines that gave an impression of the man. It was quite humble stuff, especially the part that read: 'I am Patrick, a sinner most unlearned, the least of all the faithful and utterly despised by many. Let your conclusion be that my success was due to God.' Not the sort of speech you're likely to hear on Academy Awards night.

Having been thus diverted, I followed the others into Hoban's. Even though they were quite a crowd, they'd been rapidly absorbed in the throng who, like us, had wilfully disregarded the advice in their guidebooks. Actually, most of the people seemed to be locals, so they may have been in Hoban's to escape all the tourists who'd done as they were told. Not that they seemed to mind us.

'What's your name?' one of the local women asked while I was waiting for a round of pints.

'Evan.'

'Aah now, that's a foin Oirish name.'

'Irish? I thought it was Welsh.'

'It's Celtic. It's all the same,' she said. 'What's yer surname?'

'McHugh.'

'Oh! Wid a name like dat yer one of us.'

It's that easy. Now we were friends, I asked her if she knew the whereabouts of the pub in Connemara that was reputed to have the best Guinness because they cleaned the lines with the purest water in Ireland. She looked at me as if I was completely mad.

'Now who's been tellin' ye dat. I've never hoard sooch shite in me loif. Now if yer goin' to Sligo, there's a place oive heard of that doos have the best. They've the barrels aboove the bar so it roons straight down to the taps. If it's the best Guinness yer after, that'll be the place.'

'OK. Do you know where this place is?'

'Aah. Now you're askin' me soomthin'. I could foind it on me own but I don't know as I could tell ye how to get there.'

'But it is in Sligo?'

'Yes. In the mountains behoind, near the lake.'

That narrowed things down a bit.

We stayed at Hoban's for quite some time, talking, drinking and listening to the music that started up around the tables out in the back bar. As the evening went on, the number of musicians gradually increased. Eventually the centre of the room was full of musicians with a sizeable audience seated around the walls. As more and more came in, presumably from other pubs, the number swelled to more than a dozen – eight violins, a banjo, two guitars, an accordion, a flute and a bodhrán.

Sometimes just a couple of them played. Sometimes everyone joined in, singing and playing the traditional songs. When someone got up to sing solo, the whole room hushed to pay attention.

It was a fabulous session, or would have been if Naomi Campbell hadn't kept pestering me for a dance. Eventually I had a couple of turns with her but then I insisted we had to go because we were tackling Croagh Patrick next morning.

THE NEXT DAY, the weather wasn't encouraging for mountain-climbing. The morning dawned with low grey clouds and passing showers that made the cobbles in the courtyard of the Granary wet and slippery. I could sense a degree of, shall we say, ambivalence among my little climbing party – as in, I was the only one who still wanted to go.

Twidkiwodm was the most dubious of the lot. A few months before, she'd climbed Snowdon in Wales with me – in fog, rain and wind – and hated every step. Mind you, I made it worth her while at the summit, when I stripped to my swimmers, stood on my clothes so they wouldn't blow away, and posed in my shivering skin for a photo. Such inducements not prevailing in respect of Croagh Patrick, in the end I just said, 'If you don't want to go, that's fine. But I've got a mountain to climb. A holy mountain.' It was a classic zig-zag situation. The others wanted to zig, I was determined to zag. But pretty soon, in the face of my resolve, everyone else changed their minds. Time to zag.

The base of the mountain was about five kilometres from the Granary, so we had to organise our group into little hitchhiking parties small enough to fit the average car. We did it by nationality – Australians, Italians, Germans – and spread out along the road to Croagh Patrick.

As it turned out, our hitchhiking was blessed. A woman in a van stopped to pick up Twidkiwodm and me, and being quick off the mark we realised there was room in the van for seven, even more if it came to it. As we drove towards the Italians we had to work fast. 'If it isn't too much trouble, do you think you could pick them up. They're going to Croagh Patrick, too.'

The woman hesitated but slowed down. As the boys were piling in, Twidkiwodm was pointing out the group of three Germans a short distance down the road. 'They're with us as well. There's no more after that.'

'Are ye sure? You're an army as it is.'

'We're sure.'

'And yer all going to our mountain?'

'We are. We're going to climb it.'

'Well then, if I pick them oop, will ye promise y'll say a prayer for me when ye reach the top?'

'Sure,' we chorused. No need to mention our shaky relationship with religion at this point.

Minutes later the woman dropped us off at the pub near the start of the walk, across the road from which was the National Famine Memorial. This was a metal sculpture of a bare-masted sailing vessel surrounded by skeletons flying around the rigging. As a depiction of the way starvation pursued the Irish as they fled to the four corners of the world, you'd be looking for a long time before you found a more uncompromising work. It was particularly relevant because the Great Hunger had struck hardest in the counties of the west.

Just a little way south of Croagh Patrick, in the heart of the Doolough (Dark Lake) Valley, is a scene of one of the famine's worst moments. In the middle of winter, 600 starving peasants walked from Louisburgh to a lodge in Delphi to ask for food. When help was refused, the exhausted people started their return journey. Along the way, 400 of them died of exposure and starvation.

Back over the road, the start of the path to the top of Croagh Patrick was marked by a statue of the man himself – St Patrick. He was shimmering white on a grimy pedestal, one of his hands gripping a staff and the other slightly raised. It was hard to tell whether he was giving his blessing or warning climbers to stop, go back, cease this folly. Taking his gesture as meaning the former (well, I did), we set off up the track to the summit. Not that we could actually see the summit: it appeared to be shrouded by cloud and rain. And not only that, there was a cold wind blowing in from Clew Bay. As the others complained, I took to pointing out the view while we slowly gained height and the expanse of the bay opened up below us. Dozens of islands appeared, disappearing again into the passing rain squalls. After each pause for breath and a look at the view, we kept climbing.

Croagh Patrick was a 765-metre ascent. The legend goes that it was on the summit of this mountain, around 441 AD, that St Patrick fasted for 40 days, praying for the conversion of the Irish. While there, he is supposed to have flung a bell from the summit, which was immediately returned to him by an invisible hand. He flung it again and again, and every time it came flying back. As he and God played frisbee with the bell, its sound echoed throughout Ireland and the country's entire serpent and toad populations are supposed to have heard it and fled the land. They never came back, which is almost as amazing as finding out that snakes have ears. Questions about whether St Patrick suffered from ophidophobia (fear of snakes) or whether the snakes suffered from ecclesiaphobia or tinnitus have gone unanswered. At any rate, as we climbed higher some of our party were wishing they'd gone with the asps. The path had ascended a steep slope to a saddle that ran across to the start of the summit proper. As the wind raced up the slope and tugged at our flimsy wet-weather gear, the rain squalls became more frequent. Our little expedition was strung out along the path, each of us taking the mountain at our own pace. I was starting to regret my decision to wear shorts, which I'd done because I was sure the exertion of climbing would make me hot.

St Patrick's reptilian efforts weren't the only thing that had him proclaimed Ireland's patron saint. He also played a big part in preserving religion throughout the British Isles. He was actually born a Roman Briton, in the Severn Valley near the border of England and Wales, but as a kid was kidnapped and enslaved by a raiding party from Ireland. After six years tending pigs, he escaped, found a ship and persuaded the crew to help him get away. It was pretty swashbuckling stuff for a future saint, but rather than become Ireland's answer to Errol Flynn Pat eventually fetched up off the coast of Marseille and underwent religious training in the monastery of Auxerre. He then returned to convert the Irish from their pagan ways. Less Errol Flynn, perhaps, and more Arnie Schwarzenegger.

The pagan practices that St Pat saved the Irish from included worshipping on the summit of Croagh Patrick, which had been going on as far back as 3000 BC. The success of Patrick and his disciples was nothing short of extraordinary. He and St Columba, St Brendan and many others established monasteries all over Ireland and converted its pagan kingdoms – Ulster, Connaught, Meath, Leinster and Munster. And they spread the Word to Scotland as well.

There's a point even on small mountains where your legs get so tired that the only thing keeping you going is willpower. One foot after the other, a step higher, another step. A 765-metre peak may not seem much, but the climb up Croagh Patrick starts at sea level, almost on the shore of the bay below, so you climb every single metre of the thing.

As I neared what I hoped was the top of the peak, the path disappeared into an enormous field of chunky scree that reached up and out of sight on the slope above. By now I was climbing two mountains, the physical and the personal. Horst, who lived on a mountainside, had bounded off ahead. The others had fallen behind and were out of sight somewhere below.

I continued upwards. Step, wobble, slip, climb,

shiver, balance, step. Edging slowly closer. It went on like that for half an hour. Finally, I closed on the summit… and there was a church. On the very peak of Croagh Patrick, a small chapel huddled low against the howling gale and horizontal rain. As I struggled to catch my breath, I tried to imagine someone hauling all the building materials up that mountainside: maybe it was the exhaustion, but I completely failed. Horst was huddled out of the wind in the lee of the building. Inside, we could hear faint voices mixing their song with the keening of the wind. Someone was saying a Latin mass.

Apart from the church, there wasn't much to see because the summit was completely wrapped in cloud. Visibility was reduced to a tiny cone of light that contained some bare soil, scattered rocks and a few ragged remains of what was supposed to be an Iron Age fort. Still, we felt the sense of achievement that comes with getting to the top of any peak. This one more than most – we were standing on the same spot where St Patrick had once stood. It was here that he'd allegedly given the snakes their slithering orders and prayed for the deliverance of Ireland.

WE SPENT ABOUT twenty minutes at the summit, waiting to see if anyone else from our little group was going to make it, but there was no one. As we'd promised, we offered up our thanks to the woman who'd given us a lift, suspecting they were snatched away by the wind before they had a chance to rise to heaven. Then we slowly started our descent of the treacherous slope. It was while we were still negotiating the loose rocks that we saw a small blue figure. It was some distance below, toiling upwards painfully slowly. Twidkiwodm was still slugging it out with the Croagh. Her expression was grim. She'd climb a few metres, stop and rest for a minute, climb a few metres more. When she reached us, she was completely done in – her raincoat was soaked through, her hair plastered to her skin.

'How much further?' she asked.

'You're almost there.' I almost choked on the words. There was a lump in my throat so big that I thought I'd swallowed some scree.

Horst and I followed as she laboured on up to the summit. We all have our mountains to climb and this one was obviously Twidkiwodm's. When she finally made it, she just sighed – perhaps in relief, perhaps because I'd talked her into yet another mountain and yet again there was nothing to see. While I grew increasingly nervous about what she might do to me when she recovered her strength, the clouds parted. Far below we caught a glimpse of the islands of Clew Bay – countless specks of green sprinkled across the wide sweep of grey-blue water. If not for Twidkiwodm, we'd have missed it. If not for the view, I might be dead. Talk about a lucky cloud break.

When the mist closed in again, we started down. As we went, Twidkiwodm told us she'd met a woman who was on the way down having just climbed the peak in bare feet. Every year in July, thousands climb the mountain without shoes as an act of devotion, but this woman had done it on her own. She was from Cork and had been going barefoot for months to get herself ready. 'People tink I'm goin' mad,' she'd said, 'but I'm thinking I moit not wear shoes once I'm done.'

At the bottom the others had established a base camp. They were in the pub, sitting round the fire, warm as toast. When we came in they made some space for us to thaw out, and Horst and Twidkiwodm started telling the story of our climb. I just sat and watched Twidkiwodm, the woman I still didn't know I would one day marry, as she peeled off layers of soaking wet clothing, arranging them and herself in front of the flames.

WE ALL AGREED that a celebratory feast was called for. Before we left the pub to hitch back to town, the Italians volunteered to cook and we all pitched in money for food, wine and beer. When we got back, the non-climbers went off to shop while the summiteers showered and put on dry clothes.

The others were still gone when I found a patch of sun in a small conservatory at the back of the hostel. As I soaked up the warmth like a sponge, the manager of the hostel was pottering around doing minor repairs. At one stage he asked if I'd mind holding a couple of panes of glass while he puttied them into a French window. I watched in fascination as he shaped the putty with skill.

'You could learn it soon enough,' he said, when I commented on his expertise. 'It's easy once you know the way of it.'

'I guess so,' I replied. 'It's the knowing that's the trick.'

That night, Michele demonstrated that he certainly knew how to turn out a great spaghetti. While we ate, Michael and Horst started pressing us to stay in Westport for another day as they couldn't afford to travel any further north with us. If nothing else, it meant they really didn't mind my schemes to do things like climb mountains.

Marco and Michele admitted they were in a similar position. They'd looked at their maps and realised that getting to Sligo, the next northerly town with a railway station, meant going almost all the way to Dublin and then all the way back out west again. For much of the two lines' routes across Ireland, the track from Westport ran a frustrating 25 kilometres away from the line to Sligo. Unless they hitchhiked from one line to the other, or took a bus, they'd spend an entire day on the train. It was too much travelling. If we didn't stay, they said they'd have to head back towards Dublin.

Once again, Twidkiwodm and I had to make a difficult decision. We didn't have much money and an extra day would mean we'd miss things we wanted to see further north. Since we'd already spent a couple of days with the Italians and Ulrike, we decided we had to keep moving. There was the obligatory exchange of addresses, and we ended up drinking toasts with our cheap wine and beer. We drank to St Patrick and we drank to each other. Actually, we drank to everything we could think of. When I'd arrived in Ireland barely a fortnight before, I never dreamed that I'd be sitting around a table in the far west of the country, sharing such a meal. But I also hadn't yet read a sign in one of the pubs that said: 'There's no such thing as strangers – they are only friends we haven't met.'

9

A LAND OF PUBS
AND POETS

Standing on the outskirts of Westport, I kept getting the strange feeling that I was naked. This is not an auspicious sensation when you're trying to hitchhike, but not long before we'd said yet another goodbye to all the others and now that it was just the two of us again, I was feeling exposed.

Fortunately, it didn't take long for a motorist to arrive. He told us he was going straight to Sligo. We said thanks and hopped in. As we passed quickly through the countryside, it occurred to me that Auden's little poem about poets applies very much to County Sligo and its most famous son, playwright and metaphorical poet William Butler Yeats. If it really is a poet's hope to be local but prized elsewhere, then W.B. hit the jackpot – the county of Sligo is known as Yeats Country. Not that it's easy to tell. At first glance, Yeats Country looks a lot like the rest of Ireland. It's only when you read some Yeats and see the places he wrote about that you start making connections and getting what literary commentators call 'a sense of place'.

In the town of Sligo we found a place to stay before going for a wander in the town. At the tourist office we got some information on all things Yeats, and a short distance along the banks of the fast-flowing Garavogue River we found a bookshop where I added to my slender reference library with a copy of his selected works. Yeats hardly missed a thing in his references to the land and its mythology. It was like having a guidebook that rhymed.

WHILE WE WERE wandering around I also found a relative. Researching one's ancestry is big business in Ireland, since the Diaspora has distributed generations of Irish to the four corners of the world. However, I'd never been particularly interested in delving too deeply into my family's past. I know there's a graveyard near Goulburn in New South Wales where five generations of relatives are buried, and that's about enough for me.

It was while we were poking around in the small Sligo County Museum that I saw an illuminated scroll in among the bric-a-brac of Sligo's past, dedicated to a McHugh. According to the scroll, back in the nineteenth century this McHugh had been mayor of Sligo. When he told the English what they could do with their edicts, they gaoled him – for years, it seems. When he was finally released, the locals were so impressed by his continuing resistance that they took up a collection and had the scroll made in his honour.

If he was a direct relative, it certainly explained where the family's stubborn streak came from. My grandmother was full of Brian Boru, Cúchulain and the legends. In a collection of popular poetry I inherited after she died, I found she'd hand-written a poem she thought should have been included: Yeats's 'Lake Isle of Innisfree'. My father wasn't as obviously Irish, but he was never happier than when the family was around the table eating, drinking and arguing. He was a storyteller, but not in a structured way. He had a wicked sense of humour, too. I once told a woman her eyes were as big as Kermit the Frog's. When she turned to my father for support, he just said: 'You're way out of line, son. Kermit's eyes aren't that big.'

The Sligo museum also had one of those maps of Ireland that you see on the walls of pubs all over the world, with Irish names and where they originated. I'd never taken much notice before, but now I looked up the cradle of the McHughs. I found the name just outside Sligo. What had the bus driver at Kilrush said? 'You're a long way from home.' Now, I wasn't so sure.

AFTER WE LEFT the museum we found a supermarket and decided that since we were on our own we might try to cook a romantic dinner for two. This, of course, assumed that such a thing was possible in a communal kitchen. In fact the only real problem was fending off half a dozen pairs of hungry eyes as I pan-fried two plump local trout in some butter and herbs, and steamed some potatoes and broccoli. To finish the trout, I sprinkled them with slivered almonds. I'm a regular Jamie Oliver.

We washed down the meal with a bottle of cheap French wine, clinked our glasses and drank a toast to travelling rough. Afterwards, feeling very good about life in general, we strolled into town in search of a pub, some music and a pint or two of Guinness. The man on the desk at the hostel had recommended Furey's as a place where we might satisfy all our requirements. On our way there, we were crossing the road when we had yet another typically Irish conversation. When we looked both ways for any traffic, a man promptly asked 'Are ye lost?'

'No, thanks, we're just on our way to a pub.'

'Are ye now. And which one would that be?'

'Furey's.'

'Ah, it's a foin place. Are ye sure ye know the way? Shall I take ye there? Sure it's no trouble.'

'We'll be fine. If we get lost, we'll come back and find you.'

'Well, good look to ye then.'

We crossed the street and were just passing another pub when the doors opened and out stepped... 'Marco! Michele!'

'Evans! Michelle!'

'What are you doing here?'

'We look for you. This morning we going on train.

We very sad. Then we say, is no good. We go Sligo. Find Evans and Michelle. And now we are here.'

'But what were the chances you'd find us? It's a pretty big town.' It was lucky that guy had stopped us. If we hadn't talked for a moment, we'd certainly have missed them.

'We think, look in every pub. We do this, soon we find you.'

Hmm.

FROM THE OUTSIDE, Furey's isn't the most ostentatious place. Nevertheless, most visitors do tend to pause for a moment before they enter. This is because above the name of the bar is a sculpture of Sheila na Gig. Sheila is a pagan goddess of fertility and not at all shy about it; the sculpture depicts her focusing on the means of pouring forth new life.

Inside, Furey's was a wonderfully relaxed kind of place. There were musicians playing, though it was hard to tell where the crowd stopped and the band began. In fact, from time to time members of the audience picked up instruments and joined in. We all bought pints, the boys included, and settled in for the night.

At one point, Twidkiwodm and I were standing together when the band took a break. We had an arm around each other and a pint in our free hands, when one of the band members came over to us. He was fairly old, somewhere in his sixties, with wisps of grey hair and a gaunt face. 'I'd like to sing ye a song,' he said. He then proceeded to sing unaccompanied, a ballad in Gaelic, his voice mingling with the chatter and clinking of glasses. Though embarrassed, we stood our ground as he sang, just for us.

He paused. 'This is a very old, very famous, Irish love song,' he explained, and sang us a couple more verses. A few people had stopped drinking and were starting to listen to his quite beautiful voice.

The man stopped again. 'And there's a legend,' he said, 'that as this song is sung the man will fall more and more in love with the woman.'

He sang some more. The pub was starting to grow quiet. Our skin was starting to grow warm.

'And as this song is sung,' he said, 'the woman falls more and more in love with the man.'

And he sang some more. We were now pretty much the centre of attention. He stopped again. 'And by the end of the song, the man and the woman will have fallen so deeply in love that they'll be married.'

Aaaiiieee! The M word! Twidkiwodm and I hadn't moved, but a look of horror rapidly spread over our faces. Of course, everyone in the place was now keenly interested as the man resumed singing. He was looking at us very closely and whatever it was he saw seemed to be cause for considerable amusement. Perhaps you are what you eat, in which case we were two trout, well hooked.

After what seemed an eternity, during which I broke into a sweat, he stopped again. 'Now this song,' he said, 'has thorty-two verses.' Then he started singing again. I tried to do a quick countback. How many verses were still to come before everyone in the pub forced me to my knees to propose? Curse these Irish and their pagan ways. I was trapped.

Then the man stopped singing once again and said to us in a voice that was all innocence, 'Yes, thorty-two verses. And I'll be fooked if I'm gonna sing 'em all.'

And with that he left us and headed for the bar, where a Guinness was poured and waiting for him.

THE NEXT DAY was not officially listed as Yeats Day but it was for us. We decided to chance another bus tour, having interrogated the tourist office. We were assured that the bus was small and the guides very helpful, and that they'd be stopping all over the place.

The tour was only for the afternoon, so the worst that could happen was a bad half-day. That left us the morning to explore, so we did a little Sligo walking tour. As you'd expect, this had a fair amount of Yeats connections in it anyway – the Yeats Memorial Building, the building Yeats compared to a building in Stockholm when he went to get his Nobel Prize in 1923 – plus various churches, cathedrals and hills with views of the surrounding countryside. The most interesting building, though, was in ruins.

Sligo Abbey, founded in the thirteenth century, was destroyed on the night of 1 July 1642, when the forebears of England's soccer hooligans (referred to by historians as Sir Frederick Hamilton and his troops) shot all the friars and set fire to the building. True, they may not have been interested in soccer, but an account by Yeats of what happened confirms the rest. I read this to the others while standing right where it actually occurred.

All the monks were kneeling except the abbot who stood upon the altar steps with a great brass crucifix in his hand. 'Shoot them,' cried Sir Frederick Hamilton, but nobody stirred for all were new converts, and feared the candles and crucifix. For a little while all were silent and then five troopers, who were the bodyguard of Sir Frederick Hamilton, lifted their muskets and shot down five of the friars. The noise and the smoke drove away the mystery of the pale altar lights and the other troopers took courage and began to strike. In a moment the friars lay about the altar steps, their white habits stained with blood.

I was reminded of the litany of atrocities Behan had included in *Borstal Boy*. In this place, though, the horror of what had happened was still tangible. It's no wonder the Irish find it so easy to recall the past. A town like Sligo has memorial ruins bang in the middle of town. And they're not the only reminder. Bram Stoker's relatives lived in Sligo and it's thought that their stories of the plague striking the town inspired some of the scenes of horror in *Dracula*.

Down near the docks there's another famine sculpture as poignant as the one at Croagh Patrick. It's of a mother, father and little girl, their ragged clothes fastened with rope, their heads bowed together. At their feet is a light which is used to illuminate them at night and makes them look as if they are huddled for warmth around the dying embers of a fire.

LITTLE WONDER THAT by the afternoon we were in need of cheering up. As it turned out, the bus tour of Yeats Country was everything the Ring of Kerry tour wasn't. For a start, we travelled in a mini-van, not a coach. Our driver was a fount of knowledge not only on all things Yeats but on Sligo in general. And he made his attitude to stopping quite clear from the beginning: 'If there's anything ye woont a picture of, joost sing out. I'll only ignore ye if stoppin' moit cause an accident.'

Not that we needed to do much singing out. Every hundred metres or so, there was something he thought we should photograph.

The oddest thing he showed us was at Glencar Lough. Glencar was a lake with a very Irish waterfall – or, rather, a water-up. On the far side of the lake was a cliff face with a stream flowing over it. However, the wind blowing across the lake was so strong that it took all the water, curled it back up the cliff and deposited it on the hillside above. Down below, it looked completely dry.

At the Valley of the Black Pig that cuts into the bare tabletop mountain Ben Bulben, the driver told us there was a legend that when a black pig walks down that valley the English will finally leave Ireland.

'There's been many a fella try and kick a pig down dere but so far noon of 'em have succeeded.'

When Yeats was starting out, he cut his poetic baby teeth on Irish mythology, keen on building a sense of national identity. Later he got all fired up over the tragedies of Irish history, such as the sack of Sligo. So fired up, in fact, that rather than contribute to the violent overthrow of English rule, he wrote poems, plays and essays about what had actually happened. You can imagine the consternation this must have caused. A package from Ireland arrives at the English Home Office.

'Is it ticking?' someone asks.

'No, rhyming.'

Yeats's strategy had even less impact on the love of his life, Maud Gonne, a young actor and a plotter of violent overthrow. Yeats thought she was the cat's pyjamas; she thought Yeats was a puss. Yet despite such obvious differences, Yeats proposed to Maud. She let him down with a gentle 'Never in a million years.' Not that this stopped her taking the lead role in his hit play, *Cathleen Ní Houlihan*. Written in 1904, it's regarded as the text that ultimately incited the 1916 Easter Rising. So, ultimately, it was Pen: 1; Sword: Nil.

Yeats initially disapproved of the Easter Rising, as did many of the Irish, but then the culprits were captured and shot. Yeats realised that the executions gave the Irish cause a new and powerful significance, and he captured this with the famous line 'A terrible beauty was born'. (You can see it on the sculpture of Yeats outside the Sligo County Museum, if you happen to be passing.) He turned out to be right. Pen: 1; Sword: 1.

As for our woman of action, she went to gaol for her part in the uprising (she'd married one of the ringleaders), but remained Yeats's muse for years. Which goes to show that you can't beat unrequited love for getting the literary juices flowing. Yeats eventually went into the Irish parliament, before doing the usual Irish writer's thing and moving to the continent. In Italy, he proceeded to tarnish his reputation somewhat by protesting that the Fascists weren't all that bad really. Pen: 1; Sword: 1; Hindsight: 1.

Knowing all this, we really shouldn't have been surprised by what we found at Lough Gill, where we read 'The Lake Isle of Innisfree'. Arguably his most famous work, it was inspired by the writings of the world's first hippy, Henry David Thoreau, and in it Yeats made it pretty clear he had a plan:

I will arise and go now, and go to Innisfree,
And a small cabin build there, of clay and wattles made:
Nine bean rows will I have there, a hive for the honeybee,
And live alone in the bee-loud glade.

'So is the cabin still there?' I asked the tour guide.

'No,' he said. 'There never was a cabin.'

Maybe I shouldn't take literature so literally, but for a moment I knew how Maud must have felt.

Even so, there's no doubt Yeats had a tremendous impact on Ireland in his homeland. Never mind that James Joyce is supposed to have wished he'd met Yeats when he was younger and something could still be done about his writing. That just goes to show how catty even great writers can be. The truth is that understanding Yeats may not be easy, particularly as he's a symbolist poet and everything he says means something else, but if you manage it you're well on your way to understanding Ireland.

In the setting sun, we made one last stop on our tour, to what may be the oldest man-made structures in the world. The Carrowmore megalithic tombs just outside Sligo date from 3,000–4,000 BC and form one of the most extensive burial sites in Ireland. Nearby, on the mountain of Knocknarea, is the massive tomb of Queen Maeve, who tangled with Cúchulain while trying to rustle Ulster's cattle. It's these sorts of things Yeats knew about – objects reaching back to a time that mixes Irish history with mythology and blurs the two together. But what's interesting is that Yeats doesn't come over all romantic about them. In one of his poems he describes the Tuatha De Danaan, the mythical gods who first inhabited Ireland, as 'the unappeasable host' who haunted the living. So even as he embraced his Irish past, he feared it.

BACK IN SLIGO, as evening crept into the town's streets, our immediate concern was what felt like an unappeasable thirst. Our guide's last act was to point us in the direction of Hargadon's Bar, which turned out to be a true old-fashioned Irish pub with a front bar of solid wood and a row of intimate, enclosed wooden snugs.

While we were there we bumped into the two German girls from the hostel in Dingle, Miriam and Marianne, who had fallen in with a German couple – Francesca and Hagen – travelling in a van around the Irish music festivals. After we'd been introduced and all of us had crammed into one snug, Francesca and Hagen invited us to visit a couple of pubs they'd heard about. They were in the town of Dromahair, on the shores of Lough Gill, and apparently they served the best Guinness. One of them was supposed to have its kegs above the bar, just as we'd been told back in Galway. Of course, we agreed to go.

An hour later, we were in a typical Irish country town – meaning the main street comprised mostly pubs. The first one we went into was Stanford's Bar. The barman looked quite surprised to see so many foreigners pile into the pub (with the Italians we numbered eight). He was also, to put it mildly, amused by our search.

'Are you sure you don't know a place where they keep the kegs above the bar?'

'If oid hoard of anyting so daft, oid remember. There's no place like dat anywhere near here,' he said. 'Soomwoon's pullin' yer leg.'

We ordered some pints instead, then settled around a couple of tables. While we drank our Guinness, Francesca entertained us with an impromptu performance on a small clay pipe that hung around her neck like a piece of jewellery. While she played, I couldn't help watching the only other person in our part of the pub, a man who'd been sound asleep on a stool at the bar since we'd come in. He was an old man, dressed in threadbare pants and jacket, slightly soiled. The hair on his nodding head was thinning and grey, and like so many of the older Irish his skin was deeply weathered from a life outdoors. But what was most extraordinary was that even though he was asleep he was sitting perfectly upright on his bar stool. There was a glass of whiskey on the bar in front of him and from time to time the barman came in from the other room and shouted at him: 'Jimmy. Yer dronk. Finish yer whiskey and go home, will ye.'

For ten minutes, despite the fact that the barman was yelling at him at regular intervals, we were making quite a bit of noise ourselves and the man's body was tilting first a little bit one way and then a little bit the other, he continued to sleep, kept upright by some weird, alcoholically powered internal balance.

Eventually the barman shouted louder and the sleeper woke. The moment consciousness returned, however, his balance departed and he started to topple from the stool. It all happened in slow motion, his body gripped by an unseen cyclonic wind that seemed to be trying to spin him around as his arms flailed out to grip something. Finally, a sudden gust of gravity caught him and he was on his way to the floor.

Fortunately, Michele and I were near enough to catch him as he went. I can still remember the lightness of him; his clothes seemed heavier than their contents. We lifted him back onto the stool and continued to hold him as we realised he wasn't likely to stay there for long. The barman shouted some more, 'Jimmy! D'ye hear! Will ye go home now?'

'Shlufflemuffle, arraah blemmen mubbubbl-mubble,' Jimmy replied. I don't think it was Gaelic.

'Let him be,' the barman told us as we kept hanging on. 'He'll make his own way home.'

The man didn't seem to notice our presence. All he did was reach across and pick up his whiskey. Slowly, he lifted it to his lips. He barely wet them before exceedingly carefully replacing the glass on the bar.

He took so little it made me wonder whether he was all that drunk. Maybe he was just really tired. Then, while we were still wondering what we should do, to our amazement he hunkered down within his body and went straight back to sleep. He did it as quickly as that last sentence took to read. Perhaps he'd never woken up. When Michele and I realised the man was back in the land of nod, we let go of his clothing. Sure enough, balance had returned.

WE LEFT STANFORD'S before our fellow drinker needed another sip. In Dromahair we tried a couple of other pubs, none of which had elevated kegs. They did have a good laugh though, and pints we couldn't fault, so it wasn't a total loss.

On the way back to Sligo, we passed Lough Gill once again. When I found out that the Germans didn't know the story of Innisfree or Sligo's famous poet, we stopped by the water so I could read it to them (I had the book of poems with me, as we'd adopted a 'When in Sligo, don't leave home without it' policy). A short distance from the shore there was a low bulk of land rising from the water. It could have been the island; in the dark, it was hard to tell. I explained how the poem was written during Yeats's mystical early period and how, with a few other poems of the same era, it transcended local mythology to touch a greater truth. Twidkiwodm told me to get on with it because we didn't have all night.

So I did. When I read that 'midnight's all a glimmer' it almost was. And when I read 'I hear lake water lapping with low sounds by the shore', we could. Art wasn't imitating nature, it was describing it. It was hard to tell which was stronger – the sense of place, the sense of poetry, or the suspicion that I was being a wanker.

LAST DRINKS

'What I tell you three times is true', the Bellman cried to his crew in *The Hunting of the Snark*. As we said our third goodbye to Marco and Michele in our Hunting of the Guinness, we knew it was definitely the real thing too. This was literally the end of the line for them – there were no train lines, let alone trains, to our next destination, the wild county of Donegal. So there was no way they would be able to follow us any further north.

It was hard to watch them go. At some point, we'd stopped being travelling companions and become real friends. I suspect it was when Marco and Michele crossed and recrossed the country and then searched for us in the pubs of Sligo. It was hard, too, because we knew we were commencing the last leg of our journey. It seemed such a long time since we'd boarded that ferry for Dun Laoghaire. A lot of water had passed under the bridge since then. We'd passed a lot of it, too. And the craic had been almost non-stop.

Donegal town was no different. For starters, you've gotta love a place that has a small castle in its main street. Facing the town square the order goes shop, shop, intersection, castle, intersection, shop. Did you spot the odd one out? It's not a big castle, just a pint-sized one with a couple of little towers and turrets, but it still looks out of place – like it was cold hanging out on some windswept bluff in the countryside, decided to come into town for a pint, got too comfortable, and stayed.

The castle was closed when we arrived, but we nearly had a personalised tour (of the dungeons at least) soon afterwards, when we were lucky not to get thrown into gaol for attempted manslaughter. It was while we were checking into a hostel that we noticed the manager was moving very awkwardly. When we asked why, he complained of a terribly stiff neck.

'It goes on me from time to time,' he said. 'But there's nootin' to be done for it.'

Twidkiwodm suggested Tiger Balm.

'I've never hoard of it,' he replied.

'It's not actually made from tigers, but it's great for relieving muscle pain. It penetrates your skin and warms the affected area,' Twidkiwodm explained.

'Oh, I don't think anything would work on dis,' the manager said.

A couple of people nearby overheard the conversation and put in their twopence worth.

'It's great,' they advised. 'It'll cure anything.'

The candidate for the suggested cure remained unconvinced, but further cajoling weakened his resistance. Twidkiwodm and the other woman, an Australian named Karen, helped unbutton his shirt and started to rub in the ointment.

'Do you feel it warming you?' Twidkiwodm asked.

'Yes, a little,' the man said hesitantly.

'Is it feeling better?'

'Perhaps.'

Then, he went rigid. 'Oh, oh, oh,' he went. His face paled. He swayed unsteadily and grabbed Twidkiwodm's arm to stop himself falling.

'What's wrong?' she said, not expecting quite that kind of reaction.

'The pain,' he said, as sweat broke on his brow. 'It's roit excruciatin'.'

'You'll be OK.'

'No,' he said, 'Lord have mercy. Help me sit.'

He really wasn't looking terribly flash.

'Don't worry,' Twidkiwodm said, 'you just need to rub the ointment in a bit more.'

He feebly tried to find a chair.

'Darling,' I said, 'I think he's about to have a heart attack. Would you prefer he died standing or sitting?'

'Oh, don't be so melodramatic,' she said.

It wasn't me. The manager was tottering and struggling towards the chair, muttering 'Oim dyin', oim dyin', soom water for the loove o' God.'

We sat him down, with a glass of water and watched him pant and sweat. The Tiger Balm certainly seemed to be burning bright. Slowly, however, his vital signs improved.

'Maybe we put too much on,' Karen said. 'Isn't it feeling any better now?'

'A little, maybe,' the manager said. Some colour returned to his cheeks.

'We'll leave you the tube if you like,' Twidkiwodm suggested.

'No, thanks. I'll be fine,' he said, mopping the sweat from his brow. 'I couldn't go trew dat again.'

We tried telling him that you normally get less tiger and more balm. But he preferred whatever ailed him. After what he'd been through, I couldn't blame him.

THAT EVENING WE discovered the Irish have their own cures, and far more palatable ones. We'd headed into the town centre with Karen and her son, Luke, to check out the pubs. But we only got as far as the first one we came to, McDaid's.

The bar was full of people unofficially celebrating the confirmation of their children into the Catholic Church. The reason it was unofficial was that there was no drinking allowed at the official event, in a hall across the street, so everyone was popping over to McDaid's to wet their whistles. The fact that we were mere blow-ins made no difference to anybody and we were soon invited to join in the dancing in the hall, enjoying the craic along with the best of them.

It was when one of the local men discovered that

Twidkiwodm had a touch of the flu (which I'm sure had nothing to do with our Croagh Patrick excursion) that the local cure came out. 'We've soomthing that'll fix all yer ills,' he said. 'Now wait here and I'll get the barman to mix it.' Apparently the rules about drinking in the hall didn't extend to drinking for medicinal purposes. When the man returned he had with him a tumbler containing something that looked a lot like whiskey. Twidkiwodm smelled it. 'Is it whiskey?' she asked.

'And a few other things besides. Go ahead, drink it down in woon goolp.'

She hesitated.

'Go on. It'll cure whatever ails ye.'

Where had we heard that before.

Twidkiwodm has a habit of lowering her head slightly, then twitching it to one side while she deals with a taste that's new and difficult to handle. I started to wonder where I might find some defibrillators to deal with the day's second cardiac arrest. But then Twidkiwodm took a long deep breath and smiled. 'That's the flu taken care of,' she said. 'What the hell is in that drink?'

'Ah, now. It's a simple remedy. Whiskey, hooney, lemon and cloves. Sure you can give it to everyone from the children to the old folks.'

'You give this to children?'

'Of course,' the man said.

We looked around at the kids who were dancing to the reels being played on the inevitable fiddle and accordion. They start 'em young in Donegal.

Back in McDaid's we found out that Luke was living and working in London and his mother had come over from Australia to visit him. It was her first trip overseas and she was alternately enraptured and disoriented by the sheer 'differentness' of the world around her. She constantly tried to relate things to her own experience, the better to understand them, which seemed a reasonable thing to do. After all, I've been operating along the same lines for the last couple of hundred pages.

The problem was that beneath it all Karen was, well, weird. The connections she made were weird, her past experiences were weird, a lot of the things she said were weird. The only thing about her that wasn't weird was Luke. And that wasn't just my opinion.

'She's seriously weird,' Twidkiwodm said.

'Sorry about Mum,' Luke said. 'She's a bit weird.'

'I shouldn't drink too much,' she said, as she matched us pint for pint.

Soon she thought Twidkiwodm and I were wonderful, that even if we weren't planning marriage we should because we were beautiful people and were meant for each other and we should have lots of babies because children are wonderful and Luke was the best son a mother could hope for.

'I shouldn't drink too much,' she said again, as we rationed her onto half-pints and she didn't notice. About the time she started telling Twidkiwodm but for the fact that we were in love she'd have made a move on me herself, we decided to call it a night. This took some doing.

I liked her. And Luke, but he was more in the background. We all were.

WE WEREN'T SURPRISED when Luke asked us over breakfast if we'd like a lift with him and his mother, since he had plenty of space in his car and we were headed the same way. Actually there wasn't that much space, but I suspect he had his motives. 'The more the merrier' is a very Irish sentiment. After a while, it rubs off.

Driving any distance with Karen was going to be a test on our nerves but on the other hand – the one I extended outdoors and found was getting wet – the weather had gone even softer than usual.

Most Irish people regard County Donegal as a remote and exotic place, a frontier with mythical qualities. So in many ways Donegal is to Ireland what Ireland is to the rest of the world. Not that I got far with this idea. There were only so many lulls in the stream of Karen's consciousness. Or should that be torrent? It flowed non-stop from Donegal across to Killybegs, a fishing town where we ate fish and chips on the docks, then followed the coast to Carrick with views through shafts of sunlight and slow drifting rain squalls across Donegal Bay to Ben Bulben, Knocknarea and Queen Maeve's tomb. From there it wasn't far to Slieve League, the highest sea cliffs in Europe, although the road from town was little more than a goat track. In some ways that was appropriate because the cliffs themselves were first-class goat country – over 400 metres high, twice the height of the Cliffs of Moher.

At that point I stopped worrying about Karen's stream of consciousness, because the cliffs were giving me the willies something fierce. When you lose your faith in gravity you spend most of your time walking like a duck, looking for something solid to grab hold of, rather than looking at the sweeping sodding vistas.

What was even more unsettling about Slieve League was the silence. Far below us ocean swells were rolling and falling onto the rocks. Up on top of the cliffs we couldn't hear a thing. It reminded me of David Hockney's painting of the Grand Canyon, which hangs in the National Gallery of Australia. Call me strange, but I think you can actually 'hear' paintings; they have a soundtrack. Hockney's giant landscape gets it right – the silence is profound.

North of Carrick we took a road that didn't exist to a town that wasn't on the map. Perhaps all the cartographers who went there never came back, or it may have been that the town was less residential and more fish factory. The pungent production facility occupied both sides of the main street, which was trafficked by forklift trucks moving huge bins of fish back and forth. The normal traffic travelled through as best it could, but we stopped so we could check out the fish. While we were doing so, one of the workmen struck up a conversation, telling us that the fish they were processing were mostly herring and mackerel, some crab and a few other varieties.

'D'ye want soom?' he said.

We looked at a hopper full of delicious-looking herring.

'That'd be nice. Thanks,' we replied, and started fingering some of the fish in the bin.

'Whole er filleted?' he said.

'Filleted?' Twidkiwodm suggested.

'Hold on,' he said, and went inside the factory. A couple of minutes later he was back with a large bag of filleted herring, far more than we could possibly eat. We thanked him profusely, especially since he wouldn't accept any money. He just wished us well.

Not far from Fishtown, still on the non-existent road, the countryside did actually start to manifest the sense of Donegal remoteness we'd heard of. We passed between low dark hills covered in heath, surrounded by bogs and tussocks. There were almost no houses. But like all things in a country as small as Ireland, this wild country was remarkably compact. Just as we were starting to feel like we were in the middle of nowhere, we arrived on the other side, the Pass of Glengesh. We stopped at a lookout for the view. Below us the road switch-backed down between narrow green hills that opened to a wide plain beyond. A stream ran down past neat cottages dotting the length of the valley, the fields full of grazing black-faced sheep. It was quite a jewel. For a moment, even Karen was struck silent.

It seemed that whenever we got closer to Donegal's coast the wildness gave way to farmland and small towns. But even the trappings of civilisation couldn't prepare us for an encounter with, of all things, the Statue of Liberty. Apparently, in Donegal what you're not expecting to see is often what you get. One moment we were zipping around a corner on the coast road south of the town of Dungloe, the next we were face to armpit with the iconic symbol of American freedom. It's not the actual one, but it's still a surprise. And although this Libby is a statue, she isn't as statuesque as the original – she's about two metres high, standing on the lawn of a seaside cottage facing a bay. It wasn't clear what she was doing there, but she was holding a red light. So she might have been working part-time (moonlighting perhaps) as a navigation aid. Out in the bay itself lay the island of Roaninish, upon which the film *The Secret of Roaninish* was based – a low slab of rock whose real secret may be how it could inspire someone to write about it. Was there a connection between the two? That, too, may be a secret.

I thought the bay with the town of Dungloe at its head was much more inspiring. It's dotted with rocks, tiny islands, inlets and nooks and crannies that are ripe for inspiring stories of mythical people like Selkies and mermaids. Dungloe itself was a small pleasant village with a good hostel, Greens, a short walk from the main street. Not long after we arrived, Twidkiwodm got busy with the fish and it wasn't long before we were sitting down to an early dinner of fresh Fishtown herring stewed in tomato, onion and herbs. There was so much of it we had plenty for leftovers.

Feeling well satisfied, we headed for the main street of Dungloe for a quick survey of the pubs. There was plenty of choice and after a pleasant post-prandial stroll we settled on the Triconaill Bar. When we went in and ordered our pints, the locals noted our presence then resumed muttering to each other. Meanwhile, we settled back to wait for something extraordinary to happen, as it had almost every night we'd been in Ireland.

And then…

… it didn't. No music session until the wee small hours. No late-night drive to some remote pub. No physical injuries to speak of. No apocryphal tales of superior Guinness somewhere. We waited and we waited, but it was just your average quiet night down at the local. Extraordinary. And thoroughly enjoyable to boot. I suspect we were starting to get the hang of Ireland.

THE WESTERN WORLD ends not far from Dungloe, so the next morning we went there. Beyond the little harbour town of Bunbeg we came to a rocky wilderness and a winding road that led to the northwest tip of the Irish mainland. It's called Bloody Foreland, but not because some appalling tragedy took place there. For a change, it's because there's a slight red tinge to the rocks. From Bloody Foreland you look across to Tory Island, the most northwesterly piece of Ireland. And after that it's water, water everywhere, with not a pint to drink.

As you'd expect of such a place, Tory had a lighthouse. Less predictably, it has a king of sorts and a regular ferry service, weather permitting. But unfortunately Tory was not for us. We'd reached the edge of our journey and no matter where we went we were no longer outward-bound. Europe sometimes refers to Australia as its antipodes, but for the first time in our lives we Australians knew what it meant to reach ours. It meant we were all out of pubs.

From Bloody Foreland we started heading east, towards Northern Ireland, past Slieve Errigal (2,466 metres), a high pyramid of rock and scree with white stone on its peak that looks like snow.

'Tell me we're not going to climb it,' Twidkiwodm said when we first caught sight of it.

'OK. We're not going to climb it,' I replied.

'Good. You can live,' she said.

And yet... it looked like it could give Croagh Patrick a run for its money in the holy mountain stakes. On the mountain's far side the scenic route to the town of Letterkenny would have given a rollercoaster a run for its money too. It may have been an example of the Celtic Tiger's influence not extending to the distant counties. Or it may have been that they tried to do something about the R251 but it gave the Tiger whiplash.

We stopped to rest our own necks and have some lunch just before the town of Kilmacrennan, at a pub called the Lagoon Bar. The special of the day was roast beef.

'It's very good,' the barmaid said.

'No wonder it's the special,' I replied.

'I wouldn't know about that,' she said, like I was slow.

I ordered the beef anyway. While we were waiting for our meals to come, I noticed that some people having lunch at another table had two glasses beside each plate. One glass was full of something black that looked like Guinness, the other was full of something white that looked like milk.

'Excuse me,' I said to the waitress as she passed. 'Is that milk those people are drinking?'

'Sure it is. Would ye like soom?'

'No, that's OK,' I said, 'I've just never seen anyone drink milk in a pub.'

She looked at me like it was perfectly natural to mix moother's milk with cow's milk, fool.

Things didn't improve when the roast beef came. I admit I'd said 'I'll have the roast beef, please' and just assumed that implied various accoutrements such as gravy, vegetables and sundry items that travel under the broad umbrella 'roast beef'. In the Lagoon Bar, roast beef appeared to be limited to the letter of the order – to wit, a plate of bovine comestibles and nothing else. Sure it was an enormous portion, which aroused my suspicions about whether they were trying to get rid of the stuff, but I was torn between silently tucking into what I'd ordered and underlining my stupidity further by enquiring whether I might also have condiments of some kind. Fortunately, before I got the chance the waitress returned carrying plates heaped with vegetables. 'I'll be back in a moment with your gravy,' she said. Looking at the mountain of food before me and anticipating the arrival of a vat of gravy, I realised that when they say 'special' at the Lagoon Bar, they aren't mucking around.

After a long lunch (due entirely to the time it took to consume it) we navigated the roundabouts through the city of Letterkenny and set out on the road that led to Northern Ireland. We were almost at the border when we took a short detour in order to find out what a thing called the Grianan of Aileach actually was. I thought it might be a statue of Grianan of Aileach, the man responsible for inventing most of Ireland's unpronounceable words, but it turned out to be a fort some 2,000 years old, situated on a high hill overlooking the Inishowen Peninsula. There are stepped ramparts inside and earth fortifications around it, although you get the feeling that the best defensive strategy in a place like this would be to step out of the fort when your enemies had completed the steep climb and slay them while they were still doubled over, gasping for breath.

Far below us was the island of Inch and yet more Donegal coast. Stretching into the distance was a succession of coves, headlands and sheltered waterways of Lough Swilly. As we sat and took in the view, we discussed our options. We could keep up this jogging pace and probably see all of Northern Ireland by sundown, or we could take a side-trip and spend the afternoon on the Inishowen Peninsula, spread alluringly below us. We headed for Inishowen.

Down on Lough Swilly's eastern shore, the road tracked along a sandy beach dotted with people swimming and enjoying picnics. Not having any specific plans anyway, we pulled over to dip our feet and spent a couple of hours walking and paddling in the small waves that lapped the sand. Yachts sailed by. The sun sank towards the horizon.

In the town of Buncrana, we found a reasonably priced B&B next to the town clock in the main street. If you could see your way past the graveyard at the back of the premises, there was a nice view of Lough Swilly beyond. When we headed out to dinner, we checked out the main street's restaurants, trying to pick somewhere that did light meals since we still weren't very hungry after our special lunch. While we were there I went into a bookshop where I found a collection of poems by the Northern Irish poet Seamus Heaney. When in Rome read Ovid, I reasoned.

Dinner, meanwhile, turned out to be even more interesting than lunch. For starters I didn't know that even the Chinese hadn't been able to keep the potato out of their cuisine. So with your choice of dishes you're presented with a choice of either rice or chips. So I ordered Mongolian lamb – with chips.

Fortunately there is one thing that goes well with both chips and a stir-fry, and Buncrana had plenty of pubs that sold it. The Crana Bar was probably the most interesting – it looked like it was designed by Tolkien, with a cave-like, goblin's-watering-hole ambience. The Atlantic Bar pulled a good pint and was pretty lively, though it didn't have any music that night. But O'Flairbeartaig's (O'Flaherty's) was the best of all – it had big-screen TV. We settled into a booth with some pints and Luke and I pretended to listen to Karen while we watched the football games coming in via satellite from around the world. Sport and beer. Now there's a combination that takes some beating.

LYING IN BED the next morning, I started to flick through the collection of Heaney's poems and soon understood that for a literary giant he was refreshingly easy to read. According to the jacket notes he won the Nobel Prize for 'works of lyrical beauty and ethical depth', but I thought they were muscular – meaning there was a strong, honest, workman-like clarity to the way he wrote.

As I dipped, I kept finding titbits that connected with things we'd seen. The first poem, called 'Digging', described taking milk to his grandfather, a turfcutter, for his lunch. It made me realise that the people we'd seen drinking milk for lunch the day before weren't so odd after all. Next I found 'Sheelagh Na Gig', which described a sculpture like the one we'd seen over Furey's Bar in Sligo. 'Casualty' was about pubs, poetry and Bloody Sunday, the day in January 1972 when 13 people were killed in a confrontation with the British Army in Derry, just over the border from Buncranna. 'Coffin after coffin seemed to float from the door of the packed cathedral like blossoms on slow water.' Not that Heaney was all gloom and doom. 'For he drank like a fish, Nightly, naturally, swimming towards the lure of warm-lit places, the blurred mesh and murmur drifting among glasses in the gregarious smoke' consummately capture the atmosphere of an Irish pub. I've been that fish myself. I mentioned that I take Slessor's poem 'Five Bells' wherever I go, in case I get homesick. If I was an Irishman travelling the world, of all the Irish poets I'd take Heaney.

LATER THAT MORNING we approached the Northern Ireland border with some trepidation, expecting to be menaced over passports and our intentions. We needn't have worried: when we found ourselves in the outer suburbs of Derry we realised we had left the republic without noticing any signs signifying the fact. There was no border to speak of. As anticlimaxes go, it was nothing special.

Derry says it's safe and convivial, and you can almost believe this until you see the police vehicles – armoured four-wheel-drives clad in steel, with skirts around their sides to prevent petrol bombs exploding underneath and setting them alight.

In the town itself, the police station facing Bogside is equally heavily armoured and an observation tower protrudes above the old walls of the original town. The tower has a counterbalance in the spire of St Patrick's Cathedral (where

Heaney's 'blossoms on slow water' had floated), which rises above the Bogside houses. Around Bogside, the political murals have also been maintained. These days, though, they're a tourist attraction – assuming that images of youths with firebombs, masked gunmen, and priests helping the wounded to safety are attractive to tourists.

Not far from the murals there was another reference to Bloody Sunday – a monument listing the victims. The most striking detail was their ages: half were teenagers.

FOR A TROUBLED land, Northern Ireland was still as beautiful as the rest of Ireland. Beyond Derry we drove through rolling green hills, headed for the Antrim coast and its main drawcard, the Giant's Causeway, one of the great wonders of the world.

It was squally when we arrived. A steep path led down to the seafront and the kilometre walk to the causeway. There were two ways of getting there – on foot or via a mini-bus shuttle service. Looking at the precariously steep grade at the beginning of the descent (and the prices), most people opted to leg it despite the weather.

As we stumped along, I remembered the first time I'd seen the causeway, in a picture in one of those children's 'Books of the World' that cast a wide if unpredictable net to cover various exotic locations around the globe. There were chapters on life in the Lofotens, the natives of Australia and the history of Antarctic exploration. For no good reason there was an item on the challenge of kayaking. And there was the Giant's Causeway. These days I couldn't tell you where the Lofotens are, but I knew the causeway was in Ireland. So years later, when I realised I was going there, my inner child perked up and said 'Ireland? Hey, can we go to the Giant's Causeway?'

The causeway wasn't like the book. The inner child had, of course, expected the place to be in black and white and two-dimensional. It should have been completely deserted but for some rustic fisherman giving a sense of scale as he looked out to sea. Instead, despite the wild weather, the place was swarming with people clambering all over Ireland's only world heritage site, which turned out to be made of solid rock and not paper. The rock's been there for sixty million years, when cooling lava formed polygonal (mostly six-sided) basalt columns. I have to say that, at thirty centimetres across, we're not really talking

Giant in the sense that the Grand Canyon is Grand. But then again, for all I know, at thirty centimetres the columns may actually be polygonally humungous.

The causeway has that rare quality some natural formations have, in that it doesn't look as if it was created by random forces. Like Uluru in Central Australia, it looks deliberate – like someone put it there. According to legend, it was built by a giant, the warrior Finn MacCool, who laid the pathway across the sea to get to his girlfriend on the Scottish island of Staffa, where similar structures emerge from the water.

The leader of a group of mythical warriors called the Fianna, the defenders of Ireland (Cúchulain was one of their number), MacCool also possessed supernatural powers. One of them was quirky, to say the least: apparently, whenever he sucked his thumb he became exceedingly wise. Perhaps it was a way of getting in touch with his inner child, but his warrior enemies must have given him hell.

IT WAS A dark and stormy afternoon. (I've always wanted to write that.) In between the rain squalls and the odd burst of sun we ticked off the sights –

Ballintoy Harbour, Torr Head, Carrick-a-Rede rope bridge. The more of it you see, the more you realise that the Antrim coast would be no less a place if it didn't have the Giant's Causeway. Our map was crammed with 'points of great scenic beauty' – bays, tiny villages, green fields, rugged headlands – which justified the claim that it's one of the great coastal drives of the world. And the variable Irish weather only added to it. You can keep your relentlessly sunny destinations: I'll take the dramatic interplay of landscape and weather every time.

The last place on our list was a bit of a problem, though. Fair Head wasn't accessible by car and after a long day of sights, no one else was keen to leg the two kilometres from the carpark. We'd almost certainly get soaked during the hour or so it would take to walk there and back. I looked wistfully at the map but it was pelting softness when we came back to the carpark. We sat in the car and debated what to do.

I couldn't really explain why I wanted to see Fair Head. Perhaps it was the name. Perhaps it was the knowledge that the next day would be our last in Ireland and I was looking for closure, one last adventurous experience. Perhaps it was because the edge of Scotland could just be seen protruding onto the edge of the map that told of Fair Head's great scenic beauty.

'Come on,' I said. 'Where's your sense of challenge?'

Twidkiwodm looked at me for a moment. 'It's dead. I pushed it down a ravine on Croagh Patrick.'

I got out of the car, walked around with my hands out like it wasn't raining very hard. It was no longer raining particularly hard, but the cold was as sharp as a witch's teeth. One by one, though, the others joined me. As we stumped across the heath in the wind and rain, I had to use all my powers of persuasion to keep the expedition moving. In other words, I nagged.

'Look,' I shouted over the roar of the wind, 'behind us there's a line of blue. The storm's going to pass over. We'll be in sunshine by the time we reach the head.'

'Storm?' they chorused. 'Let's go back.'

But they kept going and after 20 minutes the rain eased to a few heavy spots. A milky sunshine filtered through the back edge of the cloudline, making the wet heath glisten. Then we reached Fair Head.

Silence.

The scene was dramatic. Below us, wind-whipped

waves of blue and black were being chopped and churned in the current. In the distance they faded into the mist of an enormous curtain of rain that was gradually moving away from us. The tide was on the move and the whole ocean was flowing before our eyes, the swells rising and teetering as they fought against the current. As we watched, the sunlight around us brightened and out to sea the haze started to glow. Above us the sky was blue, cloudless, as the entire front drifted slowly over the sea. The wind was still blowing and it started to sweep away the damp, making the view increasingly sharp and clear. The sea's blue grew deeper, edged with the puffs of white caps rearing offshore. Further away still, the sombre dark grey of the squall was threaded with silver and golden shafts of light.

Then gradually, through the rain and cloud and light and dark, a deeper, darker bulk began to emerge. Slowly, almost imperceptibly, it grew more solid. A long, low stretch of land.

'It's Scotland,' someone murmured. 'The Mull of Kintyre.'

I had my closure.

THAT NIGHT WE went to a pub in the town of Cushendall, called Joe McCollam's Bar. It was the standard Irish pub – cosy front with a back bar the size of a lounge. The customers were also standard issue. Out the back there was a small party of people celebrating the birth of a man's first child. To mark the occasion the new father was dressed in a three-piece suit. He offered me a cigar. I sat back and relaxed, puffed on the stogie, sipped my Guinness and soaked up the craic.

Being in Northern Ireland, we had gone to the pub expecting we would have to be careful what we said and who we talked to. What we found was that it was disarmingly like every other Irish pub we'd been in – friendly, warm, social. When I went to the front bar to order another round, I was drawn into the usual conversation.

'Oi see yer drinkin' the Guinness,' one of the locals said. He was a young guy in overalls and a checked shirt, who looked like he'd been in a few fights.

'Yep. We love the stuff.' I was telling the truth but I wouldn't have risked telling him otherwise. All his mates, who'd heard my accent and picked my origins, were listening too.

'Sure it's foin. But ye know, the Guinness here isn't the best ye'll foind. Dere's dis place in Donegal oive hoard of. Dey've a barman… '

I put up my hand to interrupt. 'I know what you're going to say,' I said.

There was a deadly silence. To my mind the emphasis was on the deadly.

'You're going to tell me about some pub that serves the best Guinness, aren't you?'

'Oi am. You see, what he doos is… '

'Sorry,' I interrupted again. I looked around at the silent crowd. There was something I had to tell them.

'I may be a tourist,' I began, 'but in the last few weeks, everywhere I've been I've been told where the Guinness is best. In Dublin I was told that the best Guinness was put on trucks and sent to the west. In the west, I was told that the best Guinness was in Dublin.'

I glanced at the pints being poured for us. They were settling nicely, but it would still be a while before they were topped up. Not that it was certain I'd ever get to taste them. But I continued. 'In Galway I was told of a place that used the waters of a pure stream to clean the lines. In Westport I was told of a place that put its kegs above the bar so the Guinness had only a short way to travel. In Waterford, I'm sure, they'll tell you the Guinness is best served in crystal glasses. And I wouldn't be surprised if there was a place where the Guinness family goes on holidays and the best Guinness is sent there, just for them.'

The barman topped up the pints, then set them back down again. They were going to be a little longer. Time enough to dig my hole a little deeper.

'I've been to almost all these places. I've searched for a lot of them, sometimes fruitlessly and in vain (tautological perhaps, but I was spinning it out a bit). And after all that searching, I finally know where you are guaranteed to find the best Guinness. It's not in a pub two hours' drive away or twenty minutes away or even five minutes down the road. The best Guinness is in the glass, in your hand, in the pub that you're in right now. Nothing else, but nothing, compares.'

There was a pause while this irrefutable truth sank in. (No need, I felt, to mention the Guinness on the Dun Laoghaire ferry.) Then the barman broke the silence. 'Excuse me, sorr,' he said, 'allow me to shake your hond. You're the first person who's ever managed to shoot dese boogers oop.'

We shook. 'Ond yer drinks are on me. Oim sick o' dese fellas complainin'.'

Excellent. '*Sláinte*,' I said, picking up my glass. Everyone partook of the gargle. And it was very good.

OUR JOURNEY ENDED, appropriately enough, in a pub with my name on it. McHugh's was the oldest bar in Belfast, established in 1711, 58 years before the first Guinness was even brewed. So when it came to pouring a pint, they'd had plenty of practice.

We'd got to Belfast on a bus from Larne, a port where Karen and Luke had dropped us before catching a ferry to Scotland. In Belfast we'd found our way to the Golden Mile, a district between the city centre and the university that was recommended as 'relatively safe'. Relative to what wasn't made clear. Beirut perhaps.

Once we were settled in a hostel, we went for a wander. We found the Ulster Museum, where there was an exhibition of icons of Irish culture. It included Cúchulain, the Crucifix, the Virgin Mary, St Patrick, Erin, King William II, Sir Edward Carson (pro-British) and Michael Collins (anti-British).

For a city with a considerable amount of political sensitivity, it was a remarkably frank presentation. For example, one of the information panels read 'St Patrick was a British immigrant who called himself Irish and whose popular image was a fabrication.' And

276

'There never were snakes in Ireland.' This disarming honesty seemed appropriate in a way, since disarming was a continuing theme in Northern Ireland.

After the museum we took a taxi tour to see the peace line and the murals of the Shankill and Falls Roads. There was one mural in particular that struck me as odd. It quoted US President Buchanan as saying 'My Ulster blood is my most priceless heritage.' Underneath there was a further explanation: '250,000 Ulster Scots emigrated to America in the 1700s and were the driving force behind the American Revolution.'

The American Revolution? Wasn't that when the Americans threw out the British? I couldn't help thinking it was an unexpected sentiment for the Shankill Road, where every street lamp flies a Union Jack. Not that I was about to quibble.

Back in the city centre we toured some of Belfast's famous pubs, but not for research purposes. We were just interested. The Crown Liquor Saloon was built in 1885 and was a bit like Hargadon's in Sligo – lots of turned wood and snugs – except they'd gone to town with the stained glass and detailing. Not far away along pedestrianised streets (cars having been excluded to stop them being laden with explosives and parked in the city) was the Morning Star, in Pottinger's Entry. It has to be the only pub in Belfast with an Australian restaurant and such delicacies as emu and kangaroo (also demonstrating one of the best things about Australia – most of the coat of arms is edible). We had just the one pint rather than dinner, because I was eager to check out McHugh's.

I made my way to the bar and ordered what I suspected would be the last pints of Guinness we'd drink in Ireland. The pub, which was one of the biggest we'd seen, was crowded with office-workers, smoke and the roar of conversation. While I waited for the pints, Twidkiwodm managed to corner a table off to the side of the bar area. Guinnesses in hand, I edged through the crush to reach her, then slid into a seat. I set the glasses down, sat back for a moment and watched the liquid infusing in the glass. Making it last.

THE NEXT DAY we were taking the ferry back across the Irish Sea. Our adventure was coming to an end. As I watched my Guinness settle I recalled an old Arabian tale about a man who washes his face in a magic pool. As he submerges his face he experiences an entire life different to his own – full of romance, excitement and danger. It had felt the same way for us in the fleeting moment for which we'd immersed ourselves in Ireland. Yet we'd only scratched the surface: there was so much more to its music, its history, its scenery, its people, its places. I'd begun to understand why the country is such an inspiration for literature. It's a country littered with the broken pieces of a turbulent past and while the beauty inspires, the past inflames. No wonder the pens fly.

As for the woman I didn't know I would one day marry, we got married. Twidkiwodm is now known as the-cheese-and-kisses (rhyming slang for missus). It wasn't all because of Ireland (that love song in Sligo notwithstanding), but we certainly learned a few things about ourselves and each other while we were there. Fortunately the-cheese-and-kisses has infinite patience. For her part, she says she's never bored. And we learned that the perfect Guinness isn't that hard to find. You can keep your laboratories and panels of judges giving scores for colour, aroma, taste, level of hoppiness, malted creaminess and so on. Guinness tastes a lot better in Ciaran and Pat's local an hour after closing; in O'Donoghues when they're singing and the pints are crowd-surfing; in Neery's after *Borstal Boy*; in Maeve de Barra's after a thirsty day hitchhiking; listening to music in the An Pucan or the back bar of Hoban's; while being serenaded at Furey's; having a couple of quiet ones in the Triconaill; celebrating the birth of a child in McCollam's; and a lot of other places to boot.

The perfect Guinness is really just a matter of being in the right place at the right time. And what are the chances of that? Maybe one in four. But if you end up enjoying yourself so much that you forget all about searching, my guess is you've probably just found what you're looking for.

Sláinte.

Trans-Siberia

Inside the Grey Area

Paddy Linehan

£7.99 Paperback

It all started in the mind of a child with the desire to travel. Siberia was full of darkness, struggle, cold and desperation.

Years later, haunted by a shadowy image that he just can't shake off, Paddy Linehan decides to pursue his Siberian dream. He learns to think on his feet and travels 'like a Russian' in a culture struggling with post-Soviet, post-communist flux.

Traditional after-bath beatings, bonding with a love-sick Siberian boy, bizarre occurrences on the 44A Trans-Siberian train: this is an extraordinary and very human journey.

'...very cold and very far...' You almost want to go there yourself. Almost.

Fruit Flies Like A Banana

England by Canal and Classic Car

Steve Haywood

£7.99 Paperback

'A search for the soul of England? What planet was I living on? I might just as well have gone in search of a new design of wheelie bin. Or the perfect pork pie.'

When Steve Haywood hits 50, he is galvanised into action. Exploring the English canals on his trusty narrowboat *Justice*, and the countryside in his classic Triumph Herald, he attempts to delve into what it is that makes the English so, well, English. Happily mixing with the eccentric array of characters he meets along the way, Steve experiences more than his fair share of mayhem, mishaps and, of course, torrential rain.

Interspersed with the fascinating story of Tom Rolt, whose own book *Narrow Boat* inspired the founding of the Inland Waterways Association, this funny and forthright tale is summer reading at its best.

Pedals & Petticoats

On the Road in Post-War Europe

Mary Elsy

£7.99 Paperback

Christmas, 1950. Five years after D-Day, Britain was still recovering from the aftermath of war when four British girls – Mary Elsy, her sister Barbara and their friends Agnes and Esme – hatched a daring plan to give up their jobs and cycle through Europe. They would camp together in one tent on a shoestring budget, and ride 3,000 miles through battle-scarred Germany, France, Austria, Italy, Spain, Belgium and Luxembourg.

Although the Second World War was now only a memory, the ruined cities they found were a sobering reminder. At a time when few were travelling for recreation, Mary Elsy's party created a stir everywhere they went. With its fascinating cast of characters, *Pedals and Petticoats* is a charming eye-witness account of life in battle-scarred Europe.

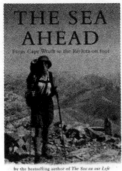

The Sea Ahead

From Cape Wrath
to the Riviera on foot

Shally Hunt

£7.99 Paperback

What would you do if you suddenly had all the time in the world?

For Shally Hunt and her husband Richard, one week at home was enough before they set off on a 2,300-mile walk from Scotland to Nice, carrying their simple needs on their backs. The couple camped wild in some of the loneliest places in Scotland, encountering searing heat in Lorraine and the Vosges and wild thunder storms in the High Alps. Along the way they met some fascinating characters, like the medium with a penchant for local liqueurs and the man who completed the Tour des Alps Maritimes on one leg.

Shally and Richard reached Nice with their sense of humour and marriage still intact – a remarkable achievement, for their journey was no ordinary walk.

Thistle Soup

Peter Kerr

£7.99 Paperback

A brimming and lively broth of rural characters, drunken ghosts, bullocks in the bedrooms and country superstitions.

East Lothian is 'The Garden of Scotland' and the setting of this delightfully idiosyncratic story of country life. Often hilarious, always heartfelt and at times sad, this memoir unfolds the ups and downs of four generations of one farming family from the northerly Orkney Isles, who move to the little farm of Cuddy Neuk in the south of Scotland just before the outbreak of the Second World War. A young Peter, the peedie boy who sets his heart on filling his somewhat eccentric grandfather's straw-lined wellies, grows up to run the family farm and become a farmer father to his own sons, putting his ability to see the funny side of things to good use, as adversities crop up with an intriguing reality...

The Worst Journey In The Midlands

One Man, His Boat and the Weather

Sam Llewellyn

£7.99 Paperback

'In order to test a wooden boat's soundness, you stab it with a bradawl. Forty stabs later, Magdalen looked like a colander. It was possible to read a paperback under her upturned hull without artificial light.'

Sam Llewellyn is attempting to make his way from the depths of Wales to far-off London. In a rowing boat.

Courageously facing the perils of the English canals, Sam and his recently repaired craft venture forth into the wettest October on record. This hilarious account of problematic weirs, eccentric anglers, and Sam's mysterious blue skin condition contains surprises and laughs aplenty as man and boat try to complete their epic month-long rowing odyssey.

Sam Llewellyn is an acclaimed author. He lives with his wife and two sons in a medieval farmhouse in Herefordshire.

www.summersdale.com